A SHORT INTRODUCTION

CW00920331

The science of psychoanalysis
During this period, it has b
offering the most profound understanding of the human mind, and
as the most effective tool for treating psychic suffering we have at
our disposal. *A Short Introduction to Psychoanalysis* offers readers an
introduction to this extraordinarily interesting discipline.

In this short volume, Giuseppe Civitarese and Antonino Ferro
explore psychoanalysis, which is at the same time a theory of unconscious psychic processes, a technique for investigating these, and a
method for curing various forms of psychic suffering, by explaining
some of its main themes and ideas. As the only introductory text to
the increasingly popular post-Bionian theory of the analytic field,
A Short Introduction to Psychoanalysis examines the theory of dreams,
the concept of the unconscious, the psychoanalytic clinic, the analysis of children and adolescents, and the history of psychoanalysis.

In seeking to give a broad idea of what psychoanalysis is, what it has
become, and the direction it may take in the future, this book will appeal
to those curious about this fascinating discipline, and is particularly
aimed at students of psychology, the humanities, and of psychoanalytic
institutes, as well as qualified psychoanalysts and psychotherapists.

Giuseppe Civitarese, MD, PhD, is a training and supervising
analyst (SPI, APsaA, IPA). He lives in Pavia, Italy. His books include
The Intimate Room: Theory and Technique of the Analytic Field; *The
Violence of Emotions: Bion and Post-Bion Psychoanalysis*; *Truth and the
Unconscious*; and *Sublime Subjects: Aesthetic Experience and Intersubjectiv-
ity in Psychoanalysis*.

Antonino Ferro is a training analyst at the Italian Psychoanalytic
Society, the American Psychoanalytic Association, and the International
Psychoanalytical Association. He is the current president of Pavia's
Psychoanalytic Centre. He received the Sigourney Award in 2007.

PSYCHOANALYTIC FIELD THEORY BOOK SERIES

The *Psychoanalytic Field Theory Book Series* was initiated in 2015. The series publishes books on subjects relevant to the continuing development of psychoanalytic field theory. The emphasis of this series is on contemporary work that includes a vision of the future for psychoanalytic field theory.

Since the middle of the twentieth century, forms of psychoanalytic field theory emerged in different geographic parts of the world with different objectives, heuristic principles, and clinical techniques. Taken together, they form a family of psychoanalytic perspectives that employs a concept of a bi-personal psychoanalytic field. The *Psychoanalytic Field Theory Book Series* seeks to represent this pluralism in its publications. Books on field theory in all its diverse forms are of interest in this series. Both theoretical works and discussions of clinical technique will be published in this series.

The series editors Giuseppe Civitarese and S. Montana Katz are especially interested in selecting manuscripts which actively promote the understanding and further expansion of psychoanalytic field theory. Part of the mission of the series is to foster communication amongst psychoanalysts working in different models, in different languages, and in different parts of the world. A full list of titles in this series is available at: www.routledge.com/Psychoanalytic-Field-Theory-Book-Series/book-series/FIELDTHEORY

A SHORT INTRODUCTION TO PSYCHOANALYSIS

Giuseppe Civitarese and Antonino Ferro

LONDON AND NEW YORK

First published 2020
by Routledge
2 Park Square, Milton Park, Abingdon, Oxon OX14 4RN

and by Routledge
52 Vanderbilt Avenue, New York, NY 10017

Routledge is an imprint of the Taylor & Francis Group, an informa business

British Library Cataloguing-in-Publication Data
A catalogue record for this book is available from the British Library

Library of Congress Cataloging-in-Publication Data
Names: Civitarese, Giuseppe, 1958- author. | Ferro, Antonino, 1947- author.
Title: A short introduction to psychoanalysis / Giuseppe Civitarese
    and Antonino Ferro.
Description: Abingdon, Oxon ; New York, NY : Routledge, 2020. |
    Series: The psychoanalytic field theory book series | Includes
    bibliographical references and index.
Identifiers: LCCN 2019043745 (print) | LCCN 2019043746 (ebook) |
    ISBN 9780367415488 (hbk) | ISBN 9780367415501 (pbk) | ISBN
    9780367815165 (ebk)
Subjects: LCSH: Psychoanalysis.
Classification: LCC BF173.A25 C58 2020 (print) | LCC BF173.A25
    (ebook) | DDC 150.19/5—dc23
LC record available at https://lccn.loc.gov/2019043745
LC ebook record available at https://lccn.loc.gov/2019043746

ISBN: 978-0-367-41548-8 (hbk)
ISBN: 978-0-367-41550-1 (pbk)
ISBN: 978-0-367-81516-5 (ebk)

Typeset in Bembo
by Swales & Willis, Exeter, Devon, UK
Printed and bound by CPI Group (UK) Ltd, Croydon CR0 4YY

CONTENTS

INTRODUCTION

Written jointly by its two authors, this book aims to provide an elementary introduction to psychoanalysis. Recently, the science invented by Sigmund Freud – which is at one and the same time a theory of unconscious mental processes, a technique to investigate these very processes, and a method of treatment for various forms of mental suffering – passed the century mark. This is not a long time compared to other disciplines, yet during this century, psychoanalysis has achieved a great deal and has established itself as the instrument that provides us with the deepest knowledge of the human mind; on this point there can be little doubt. The scientific, philosophical, and cultural impact of psychoanalysis is so self-evident that it is almost superfluous to point it out, and seeking to give an exhaustive account of it is undoubtedly a huge task. Inevitably, the choice of what to focus on can only be left up to our subjectivity and our preferences; for example, great emphasis will be placed on clinical practice at the expense of other interesting but more abstract aspects. This will inevitably lead to gaps and repetitions, for which we apologize. The former will be due to obvious limitations of space, the latter to the fact that certain questions will only be touched on briefly in some chapters and then later expanded on or looked at from different angles. This book seeks to give a broad idea of what psychoanalysis is, what it has become and the direction it may take in the future. Our main aim is to arouse curiosity in the history and present state of an extraordinarily fascinating discipline; this book is aimed at younger readers – those still attending high school as well as the many students at the faculties of Psychology and Medicine, whose university courses fail to provide answers to their questions. With this in mind, at the end of the book, we recommend some further readings, concentrating mainly on the works that are most easily available for those wishing to explore, in depth, the subjects discussed. We also list some websites addresses, where the reader can find further information as well as research and work tools.

As it would be impossible to do justice to all of the many important concepts and authors that have shaped both the historical development and current state of psychoanalysis, we have chosen to adopt a horizontal rather than a historical approach (except when this is essential to understanding).

The first chapter provides some general information, also of a practical nature, to help readers get their bearings as they get to grips with psychoanalysis.

The second chapter is organized around the concept of the unconscious, which is seen as a kind of *shibboleth* in psychoanalysis – or in other words it's most distinctive or characteristic feature. The unconscious psychic processes are indeed the starting point for dealing with the enigma of disturbances that otherwise would elude understanding and treatment. We have made the deliberate (and painful) decision to limit ourselves to the five authors who we think have made the most original contribution to shaping and developing the concept of the unconscious (leaving aside Jung, who, for historical reasons, split off from the Freudian movement and founded another school): Freud, Klein, Winnicott, Lacan, and Bion.

The third chapter focuses on dreams as an access route to the unconscious functioning of the mind and as a paradigm of clinical work. We also present various clinical illustrations to explain how the way of working with dreams has changed in everyday clinical work.

In the fourth chapter we then go on to look at the main instruments of treatment – the contents, as it were, of the analyst's toolbox.

The next chapter (Chapter 5) which focuses on child and adolescent analysis is important for various reasons. First of all, this is a fundamental area for the treatment of mental suffering and for the prevention of the most important psychiatric disorders. For some years now, for example, the use of psychoanalysis in the therapeutic treatment of the couple made up of the mother and the newborn child, has represented a pioneering intervention. Secondly, because the extension of analysis to children has been at the origin of the great theoretical renewal of psychoanalysis, a renewal that has also become a model in adult therapy. In the foreground, for example, stand the non-specific aspects of treatment centred on emotional understanding, while receding more into the background are the more specific aspects of interpretation, such as the uncovering of the unconscious functioning of the psyche. We have come to realize that all too often the kind of interpretation that sought to clarify to the patient the meaning of symptoms and the way in which their unconscious produces them, often has the effect not so much of emancipating him but rather results in subtly feeding the narcissism of the analyst on the one hand, and the patient's sense of guilt on the other, leading him to think: "I'm in a bad way, I'm a bad deal; and what's more I am hard and obstinate, I do not want to understand". What matters more, however, is the sharing and the containment of emotions.

In the last chapter (Chapter 6), we touch on the rather bewildering problem of the multiplicity of psychoanalytic models, and in this context we briefly explore the history of Italian psychoanalysis. Finally, while in the body of the book we provide a short definition of technical terms as they are introduced, to make things easier, at the back of the book readers can also find a brief glossary that brings together some of the main concepts of psychoanalysis most frequently referred to in the text. The first occurrence of each of these terms is marked with (*).

WHAT IS PSYCHOANALYSIS?

Psychoanalysis is the most effective tool for treating psychic suffering we have at our disposal. Initially, its field of operation was rather limited, so much so that it was necessary to "test" whether the patient met the criteria of "analysability", that is, whether he/she was suitable for the "talking cure", as Freud called it. Since then, definitions of what can be treated by psychoanalysis have greatly expanded to include ever more serious pathologies that were initially excluded, such as borderline, psychotic, psychosomatic patients, and so on. In these cases, therapy is accompanied by psycho-pharmacological treatment, preferably prescribed by someone other than the analyst. The strength of psychoanalysis, as well as its prime instrument, lies in what is also its limitation, namely, the analyst's mind in contact with that of the patient.

In the early years of the history of psychoanalysis the analyst was required to be utterly neutral, that is, he was supposed to listen in an active but detached way. Gradually, however, the value and importance of his mental functioning and the relationship that is established with the patient in the analytic situation came to be acknowledged.

As we know, we owe the discovery, or perhaps we should say the invention, of psychoanalysis to Freud's genius. It was he who identified its three pillars that remain valid to this day: the concept of the unconscious, the role of sexuality in psychic development, and the dream as a means of access to the inner world of the individual.

Initially, the unconscious was described as the place inhabited by the drives, by magmatic proto-emotional states, by everything that was not accessible to consciousness. To explain the psyche, Freud then elaborated the concepts of ego, id, and super-ego. For a modern metaphor we might turn to the television series *Wayward Pines*. The main characters live in a town, bearing the name Wayward Pines, that could represent the ego, protected by an electrified grid that keeps out primitive monsters. If these primitive monsters could get in, they would destroy the town. These primitive monsters could be broadly equated with the id, while the super-ego would be the seat of moral instincts.

OLD AND NEW LANGUAGES

Currently, psychoanalysis finds itself midway between old and new languages. Many are trying hard to understand and reveal the relationships between them, asking the question, for example, "What are the differences between ego and alpha function?" In our view, however, this is a futile and perhaps even damaging exercise. No one today, talking about metapsychology★ (the study of how the mind is structured independently of the phenomena that consciousness experiences), is thinking only of Freudian theory because the theories of Klein, Bion, and the theory of the psychoanalytic field etc., have become an integral part of psychoanalysis.

The lexicon of early psychoanalysis was more militaristic in origin: defences, resistances, drives, mechanisms were put in place by the patient for protection and to keep the analyst at bay, who was regarded as a neutral mirror, a sort of archaeologist whose task it was to reconstruct the patient's history, especially as a child. This is, for example, what we see in the Alfred Hitchcock's (1945) film *Spellbound*, where the discovery of a childhood trauma frees the main character from his anguish and fears. Subsequently, as more importance became attached to the relationship between analyst and patient, and what happens unconsciously between the two, new expressions were introduced, such as attacks on linking, projective identification★ and unconscious fantasy. Now we have reached totally different languages, much less saturated, less definite, and with a wider-range of shades of meaning:

alpha function★ (something we know little about, a function of the mind that is capable of transforming primitive feelings and emotions into pictograms or mental images), alpha elements (more advanced stages of pictograms), beta elements★ (sensoriality itself), negative capability (the ability to be in doubt without being overwhelmed by a sense of persecution and the preference for involuntary over voluntary memory), and selected fact (the element chosen to give meaning to a given event in analysis after a sufficient period spent in a state of negative capability). These new formulations have gradually given rise to a new theory of the mind in which tools for thinking count more than the past, childhood, the historical reconstruction of the patient's biography, the systematic exploration of sexuality, and the identification of the trauma. Now, work tends to be done less on content and more on the functioning of the various apparatuses and tools used for thinking. It's just like someone in a kitchen moving away from an interest in what is in the refrigerator or in various shopping bags, to making sure that all the cooking utensils work well: from the pots and pans to the vegetable mill, from the food processor to the gas rings, also including everything that is needed to transform raw food (proto-emotions and proto-thoughts) into actual dishes (emotions and thoughts capable of containing and expressing emotions and complex mental states).

The aim of analysis is to precisely develop these utensils and a psychic "container": the ability, that is, to give meaning and form to rawer emotions and feelings; the ability to amplify the oscillations between the paranoid-schizoid position★ and the depressive position★ (expressed in the jargon as PS↔PD), in other words, between disordered primitive creativity and the ability to integrate.

This inevitably sends us in the direction of a bi-personal (or rather group) metapsychology. In practice, the analyst no longer regards himself as neutral but rather as fully involved in the analytic relationship. Analysis becomes a sort of shared staging – precisely what is expressed by the concept of enactment. In modern psychoanalysis it is accepted that the analyst can sometimes say something about himself (so-called self-disclosure). These new ways of thinking about psychoanalysis emphasize the importance of the relationship, the use of daydreaming to intuit what is happening between analyst and patient on a deep emotional plane and the joint construction of meaning. Equally, however, other factors are also important, such as the number of hours the analyst has slept and the quality of his mental functioning.

Inevitably, all this flows into a radically intersubjective view of analysis and into the ineluctable concept of "analytic field", that is used to describe this type of interpersonal functioning. From the field perspective, the two-person "relationship" is expanded to include all of the characters, all of the different types of atmosphere, all of the shadows that spring to life in the consulting room. Progressively, a process of selection takes place: the casting of the characters best suited to indirectly recount the emotions that are ignited in the emotional field. They can be characters from the human, animal, vegetable or mineral world, but also abstract concepts, etc. It is therefore crucial for the analyst to develop his capacity for dream thought in the session.

A fragment of biography, a realistic story, a film seen, a lived experience, a childhood memory, an event – these all lose their status as reality and become "characters" within a virtual reality that coincides with the intersubjective dream field.

Compared to the past, this field is much less something to decipher and decode and far more the locus of possible narratives and transformations that constantly enlarge the field itself. In this case, "field" refers to the amplitude and depth of personal meanings that can be attributed to a lived experience. The split-off parts of personality, the not yet thinkable – or only potential – identities come to life and become "narratives" in the consulting room. What becomes important is the development of tools to contain, think, and feel; equally important though, are the transformations that cannot be narrated to those that can be depicted and then put into words. To put it another way, the "stone" of dehydrated and compacted emotions exposed to the oneiric lithotripter (the instrument that crushes gallstones) is broken up and rendered narratable in its newly found emotional components.

Also, sexual discourse is "listened to" as an unconscious and allegorical way of talking about relations between minds or between minds and emotions. There is no communication that, in principle, cannot be heard in terms of its overall value, as unconscious and belonging to the field – in other words, as intersubjective.

The modern conception of psychoanalysis attaches great importance to the patient's right not to be confronted with interpretations that sound bizarre or intrusive. He should have the right to see his story accepted and shared, while at the same time the analyst should remain aware that the field (to repeat: at one and the same time the dynamic magnetic resonance imaging of the emotional forces in play and a structure that generates meaning) "evolves" all the more the less we disturb it.

Thus, there is a shift in interest from the journeys which are typical of the classical model of psychoanalysis within the worlds of Oedipus, the primary scene, primary destructiveness, libido, and castration anxiety, towards the new open spaces represented by the field of analysis up to "nurseries", where not only the most primitive nuclei of the mind (typical of psychosis, borderline or disturbed personalities, and psychosomatic disorders) become narratable but also scantily treated traits, such as autism or Asperger's, whose characteristic quality is precisely the inability to tolerate change.

At this point in our zigzag course through time, we once again run into the unconscious, which now becomes the metabolized version of facts, of the real – that is to say, dreamed reality is rendered unconscious, producing an unconscious that is seen as extremely vital and in transformation. In the current conception, the unconscious is continually formed from *beta* elements (sensoriality) after they have been transformed into *alpha* elements (pictograms). The direction taken by the analysis is no longer from the unconscious to the conscious, but from the conscious to the unconscious. In other words, it is no longer a question of translating and explicating the unconscious dynamics of the patient but rather of ensuring that his ability to give the fullest possible meaning to experience becomes direct and automatic.

This is what happens when you learn to ride a bike, to play an instrument, or to use a keyboard: after a while, you stop thinking about it, you can do it with your eyes closed, automatically.

There is another difference in and between the two languages of psychoanalysis (classical and contemporary, at least the contemporary version that we feel is most alive and effective): the former tends to celebrate what is already known and suggests the existence of broad, organized knowledge; the latter presents itself as provisional, fragmentary, and (mildly) sceptical. Also, it is there to constantly give the measure of what we do not know, pointing more towards the exploration of the unknown.

DOES PSYCHOANALYSIS HEAL?

The sole and final purpose of psychoanalysis is to heal. It makes no sense to think of psychoanalysis as if it were some kind of mystical, esoteric, or cognitive path towards enlightenment. Basically, the "miracle" it performs is the relief of psychic suffering. Symptoms, "re-dreamt" by patient and analyst, in other words rendered significant in some way, are transformed into images, narratives, and dreams that make for a less troubled and more harmonious mental life.

WHO IS ANALYSIS FOR?

The common factor that unites all those who seek analysis is a certain degree of mental suffering. In certain situations this is made explicit: a person asks for an analysis because they find themselves in a clearly depressed state or in a situation of discomfort in their family or because they are prompted to do so by obvious symptoms such as panic attacks, phobias, obsessive rituals, all-consuming anxiety, etc. Others are not able to enter so directly into contact with the changing and at times masked expression of their suffering and use some kind of ploy. For example, analysts hear people say, "I want to do analysis because I am a psychologist, because I am a psychiatrist, etc." They too are bearers of suffering, but they hide it behind a request for treatment on cultural or professional grounds.

A problem that often faces those who want to enter into analysis is the cost of therapy, because today, and we believe still in the near future, in Italy, psychoanalytic therapy is almost exclusively available to private patients, meaning that the individual has to bear the costs. It is true that many analysts now offer analysis at affordable rates – there is no comparison with how things were years ago – but the fact remains that the cost is high. This problem is also connected to geographical region. The situation is different in Nordic countries, and in Germany and Switzerland, where, for a certain number of years, psychoanalysis is paid for, at least in part, by the national health system. In other cases, when analysis is prescribed as the chosen therapy for a given disorder, the cost is borne entirely by the State.

After all, in the face of significant levels of psychic suffering, what alternatives do we have? We can take the route of psycho-drugs, for example, in the case of depression following a traumatic event, or in panic situations, which are also connected to life events. However, psycho-pharmaceuticals are often also prescribed alongside analysis. In the past, this problem was debated together with the famous question of the criteria of analyzability that established whether a particular patient with a particular pathology could be treated using analysis. The idea was that neuroses★ were the elected object of therapy and it was essential that patients should be of a certain "intellectual" and cultural level. Today, the "pathologies that can be analyzed" may also include borderline and psychotic disorders which involve productive symptoms such as hallucinations and delusions as well as psychosomatic pathologies.

In short, rather than posing ourselves a nosographic-diagnostic problem, what we now do is simplify the type of problem as far as possible.

At most, we try to distinguish between:

- suffering involving a level of sensoriality that goes beyond what can be metabolized using normally developed mental functions;
- suffering where the containing functions of the mind are lacking;
- suffering where there is an excess of sensoriality which cannot be contained or transformed and is therefore evacuated (hallucinations and delusions) into the body (psychosomatic disorders) or affects intelligence (learning defects);
- suffering from severe or very severe deficiency of the weaving and metabolic functions of the mind (autistic spectrum).

It should be noted that this gradient also implies significant differences in analytic technique.

Often, psychic suffering is manifested through the multiple pathological defence mechanisms to which the subject★ resorts unconsciously.

We possess an almost infinite number of such mechanisms. To give some examples of this type of situation:

- the projection★ of one's own needy parts onto an "other" (who accepts this) and the forced caring for this "other". In this sense the "other" is that which is not recognized as a part of oneself (for example, H. cannot separate from F. with whom he does not seem to have much in common because he thinks that F. would not be able to survive "alone", but then later declares himself astonished when F. says she will find a job somewhere far away if they separate);

• or negation through the erotic excitement guaranteed by a young lover who often becomes a card people play in certain depressive situations, because it allows them to go back a number of squares in the existential game of snakes and ladders. Compared to one's companion in a life that often bears all the hallmarks of harsh reality, the young lover acts as a drug, a stimulant and a painkiller. Often this is another suffering person and looking after them serves many purposes at the same time.

An example might be the character Italia, wonderfully played by Penélope Cruz in the film *Don't Move*, based on the novel of the same title by Margaret Mazzantini (2004).

A patient, Stefano, turns sixty, a point in his life that coincides with a change in his work situation. So far he has only been interested in his family – he is married with four children – but then he falls in love with a young girl who brings out in him feelings of mad jealousy that take up the whole of his mental space and deflect him from his depressive pain. It's like going off on holiday to another galaxy of existence where you are no longer recognized, but by doing so you step away from time and pain.

Sometimes, though, there is a sudden and harsh awakening – "Where am I and what am I doing?" – which is accompanied by a feeling of total estrangement and the urgent need to return to one's own reality, however painful it may be. Other times, however, a person feels captured inside a bubble whose walls are lined with film images, like a kind of Truman Show, where awakening is a long, slow, progressive process which involves a constant coming and going between these para-hallucinatory bubbles and reality. In other cases, again, it is seeing or perceiving something inconsistent in this para-reality that prompts suspicions as to "where" one has ended up and why.

For Stefano, for example, seeing the friends who surrounded the person who, for him, had become a sort of idolized Rita Hayworth prompted a progressive awakening. A den of thieves made up of friends of both sexes who turned him into an observer of how different his dream was from reality. In fact, to be exact, the first cracks in his film with Rita Hayworth were the lies that began to create rifts in this highly idealized situation. Gradually, Stefano manages to wake up from his dream, but after paying a high price in terms of disappointment, jealousy, disorientation, and loss of the coordinates of his life. Raw emotions, over-the-top outbursts, and repeated lies lead him to recognize the "emotional brothel" he has fallen into – like some kind of latter-day Professor Unrat.

Professor Unrat is a paradigmatic figure of this mode of functioning, through which he and Rosa Fröhlich are brought to the tragic destiny that plays out in the unforgettable ending of Heinrich Mann's masterpiece (*Professor Unrat,* English title *Small Town Tyrant)*.

The notion that people provoke harm to ward off psychic pain is one of psychoanalysis's most obvious and widely shared psychoanalytic insights; and the range of possible enactments is astonishing.

Very often, the depressive suffering that lies at the origin of psychic suffering is due to an inadequate method of organizing, metabolizing and containing the clumps of feelings, or proto-emotions of abandonment, loneliness, and persecution with which are filled and are reflected in children's fables.

What differentiates the art of listening as practised by an analyst from that of a friend or family member? The analyst has many more tools than a friend or family member and these enable him to understand the possible deeper and more structural reasons that mark the way that a particular person functions and that cause his or her suffering. His toolkit also contains "lenses" for diagnosis and "scalpels" for working more deeply on the signs of suffering that emerge in the consulting room.

RELIABILITY

Analysts are psychologists or doctors who have specialized in clinical psychology or psychiatry and then gone on to take a long training course (a kind of second postgraduate course) that includes a personal analysis, years of theoretical lessons, clinical seminars, periodic tests of the progress made and years of supervisions relating to personal cases. People come to the profession of analysis relatively late in life and usually after having accumulated extensive clinical experience in a wide variety of different areas of mental health. Training is also an ongoing process. It is impossible to imagine an analyst who is not actively involved in the scientific life of the institution to which he belongs.

There is therefore a body of information that an analyst should know before embarking on an analysis or psychoanalytic treatment. Good practice dictates that you turn to someone who has already completed a proper training path. Just as we can check whether a person is actually a physician by looking at the list of registered doctors, similarly, we should inquire about the training and theoretical orientation of our chosen specialist; in short, we should check that he or she is a certified professional. In the United States, it is established practice for psychoanalysts to have their own website on the Internet and to keep a copy of their curriculum vitae in their practice for patients to consult, so that they know who they are dealing with.

In Italy, there is often an attitude of mistrust towards psychological therapies, but we believe that in a sense this is quite legitimate. While it is relatively easy to understand which heart specialist is good and which is not, unfortunately, in the field of psychotherapy, primarily for historical reasons but also due to the complexity of a subject that is not easy to standardize, there is a much greater range: you can find practitioners who are capable or incapable, well-qualified or completely unqualified. Obviously, in our field, it is more difficult to get it right straight away, that is to say, to find a professionally qualified, honest, human, and experienced person, someone with whom one can get along with relatively well. For our part, we would suggest using a very simple evaluation parameter: one should see if one feels understood and relieved from the very first session, that is, if one comes out of it feeling "lighter" than when one went in. This is already an indication that something good is happening.

An analyst who never talks, who systematically refuses to answer questions, who seems to have come out of a Hollywood movie, would be more at home in a joke about psychoanalysis than in reality.

In the long run, but perhaps even in the short term, one should have the feeling that the therapy one is undergoing is of some use, that new scenarios are opening up, even if initially they may be frightening or disturbing, and that ultimately one feels better.

Outside the consulting room one could imagine a sign saying "Laundromat". In other words, one enters with dirty clothes, puts them in the washing machine and then one goes out with clean clothes. Sometimes, some stains will remain, but overall, the wash should have produced satisfactory results.

THE PROBLEM OF THE FREQUENCY OF SESSIONS

Given the hectic nature of modern life and people's average level of income, the idea of asking someone to do three or four sessions a week is not that easy; that notion seems to belong to another age. It is undoubtedly true that a full analysis seems to have become a luxury for the few. Nonetheless, we believe that sometimes a person can ask for treatment that is "psychoanalytic in type", in other words, something easier for the patient to cope with, with one or two sessions a week. A person may also find an analyst willing to charge moderate prices, which makes it possible to work at a more intense pace.

Increasingly, psychoanalytic-type interventions are deployed, and excellent results can also be obtained with fewer sessions using the standard psychoanalytic tools. In this case, some parameters of the setting can be waived, but the central principle of a certain type of listening that only psychoanalysis can produce is maintained. The difference may not be enormous, as long as the patient's suffering is not too severe. From an analyst's perspective, however, the ideal is to work with several sessions a week, because this makes it easier to bring about a general restructuring of personality. It's like calling a plumber because a radiator is leaking. Of course, it would be nice if he said, "Let's redo the plumbing throughout the whole house. Then I can guarantee that everything will work well for the next twenty years". However, this is not always feasible and is not always the sensible thing to do. Often, it is enough to fix the radiator and perhaps six months or two years later to do some extra small work on the leaking water heater, and so on.

Our culture pays greater recognition to physical suffering; when it comes to mental suffering, it is much easier to say, "Yes, but what's important is a person's will, their commitment" – as long as you are not the person affected. When someone begins to suffer from panic attacks we don't seriously ask the question: "What are you afraid of?" Rather we play things down. And faced with someone who has a serious hypochondriacal disorder, it would be superficial to say: "It's no big deal", or to suggest "Get over it", to someone who has a severe phobia.

The fact is that psychic suffering presents the same gradient of pain as any other suffering. Although it is often too late, it is easy to register when it reaches levels that prevent normal living.

THE ARRIVAL OF A PATIENT

When a new patient knocks at an analyst's door they should be welcomed in a spirit of maximum readiness to listen, whatever they have to say. Generally, we show him into the consulting room, offer him a seat and perhaps say something to help him feel at ease, for example: "So?"; or, even without asking, using facial expressions or some sound or other, we invite him to talk about what has brought him there.

For example, the person we meet might tell us that he feels as though he were only living half a life: his days flow by but he doesn't really feel involved in what he is doing. The first thing a good psychoanalyst should do, of course, is to listen, and then later try to work out what is happening to the patient, perhaps trying out metaphors to see whether they chime in with the latter's experience. If the experience conveyed by the metaphor matches that of the patient, it's as if what we see on a cell phone display is projected onto a larger screen, perhaps from a new unexpected angle of vision or with a fresh sharpness of focus.

In order to shed more light on things, we might ask the patient about his feelings when looking at the sea: does he see everybody diving in, swimming around, having fun, splashing each other with water, fighting or hugging while he is still on the beach, at most perhaps paddling but never really entering the water; or, one might use a horse metaphor. For example, one might ask whether he feels he is holding the horse with a tight bridle, almost walking, while alongside him others are trotting or even galloping. It is always necessary to monitor whether these metaphors help to embody the patient's experience in an image, or not. If the patient does not enter into this experience, we should adjust our aim. We need to be able to find metaphors that the patient feels resonate with what he has said.

The patient's experience of not really being able to live could also be rendered in the image of someone who never manages to play the game, who is more of a spectator of his own life rather than a player. Of course, watching a football match rather than playing it gives you more of a feeling of being protected, though it would be more enjoyable to play. If you play you also get kicked and if you have been kicked in the previous game you're justified in saying, "I'm just going to watch for a bit before I go back on the pitch". Let's take another example.

Let's imagine the story of a 15-year-old who comes to us because he has been accused of raping a 13-year-old girl. The boy describes how he kissed her, his feeling that she seemed to be up for it, although he doesn't have a very clear memory of what happened; it appears he abused her even though he remembers her giving full consent. When he wakes up the next morning, he is arrested, an event that traumatizes him and leaves him perpetually reliving the nightmare.

The point of this example is to explain how different types of psychoanalytic listening work.

An analyst who takes a more classical approach would think of this situation as a traumatic event with all its consequences, an event that has to do with adolescence. According to the model of the analytic field, on the other hand, the therapist would take a different approach: he would be on the boy's side in relation to the problem he is describing, in other words, the anguish he felt because of what he had found himself doing without being aware of it (he had understood that he had been given the green light, and had carried on, but he had read the traffic light wrong: it was amber). His is the anguish of not knowing how to decipher the signals (if you tell me "yes" and then we have sexual intercourse, and then you accuse me saying it was a "no", that I didn't understand, that the traffic light was not green but red, then it's as if I shouldn't have been driving the car).

At any event, the main thing is always to share the story with the patient, to talk about what he tells you: you have to play the game of chess that he proposes, with the queen, the king, the castle – but also with other pieces, because he might in fact bring along more than just the standard ones. You must use his language and above all you must let that language develop gradually.

To come closer to the patient's language, during the session we might even imagine a story about a famous anthropologist, Lévi-Strauss, who happens to have a brother called Strauss-Kahn (the French politician accused of raping a maid in a New York hotel). It might be the story of a decent person who is sometimes, unbeknownst to himself, possessed by this secret relative of his (a kind of Mr or Mrs Hyde), a violent, insidiously intrusive part of himself that has basically raped *him*. He finds himself in the role of the victim, having been abused by an alter ego of whom he was totally unaware.

We can use different images every day because analysis varies from day to day. During the first session, we might think that we are having to deal with extremely violent emotions that have been met coldly or with bear-like emotions that are being held in check by hibernation. But we know that this bear may occasionally wake up, and when it does the whole community is in trouble. The problem in such cases would not be how to kill the bear, but how to tame it without making it look ridiculous, as would be the case if the bear were forced to dance; we have to train it only so much so that it doesn't send the town into panic. That is to say, it should become a sufficiently domesticated bear, so that we always know where it is and how it can be handled. Then we will see this bear's story, where it comes from, why it has developed to such an extent, what kind of treatment it has received that has made it so "bear-like" (the word "orso" in Italian refers to a grumpy, anti-social person). In the consulting room we have a well-behaved fifteen-year-old boy to deal with – but also a bear.

If we are afraid of bears, then we should tell him we have no room for him and recommend he go to a colleague we know to be a good bear-tamer. But bears don't scare us, so we take him on for analysis.

ARE DREAMS ALWAYS CENTRAL?

Much has changed about the way we understand dreams in psychoanalysis. Once it was thought that the patient's associations were needed in order to interpret dreams, that the patient's "reading" of them was necessary. Later, we began to realize that the key lay in what the patient said before or after the dream, and then in the interpretations that occurred to the analyst. This whole situation has now been reset, as it were, and many of us now consider dreams as densely poetic communications that need to be not so much interpreted as intuited or sensed, as we would do with a poem (either you get it or you don't; just like when a trapeze artist flies into the air – either he is caught or he falls).

We would like to add that the interpretation of dreams is not a magical operation, something that can be offered to the patient independent of thought. Aside from the various factors that guide intuition, such as the spontaneity that only the analyst's experience and talent can provide, the most important thing is the validation that the patient himself gives consciously, but above all unconsciously, to what is proposed as an interpretation. Sometimes this must be presented in diluted form, sometimes in concentrated form, but it should always be a kind of buffet, never imposed, never force-feed. It must be offered in such a way that everyone can take what they need. This is a key parameter in the dream validation process.

The same dream could also mean different things on different days or in different contexts. If someone wishing to be taken on as a patient came to us telling us that he was very alarmed, and had anxious feelings that were not proportionate to reality – for example, if she says that she lies awake all night every time her son has an exam; or if she talks about her daughter going out with a boy, and that this causes her great anxiety because she doesn't know who he is, whether he is trustworthy or dangerous – we would always have to distinguish between what we share with the patient and what we hold in our minds in some way or another. This will serve as a provisional framework for our analytic work – which obviously might always change the next day. Each time we have to start from ground zero, each time the story will be completely different.

Another step we try to take is to see how patients' communications can be understood outside the dream and what its meaning might be. For example, if at a certain point a patient talks about having seen a documentary by Hitchcock about what was happening in Nazi Germany even before the establishment of concentration camps, the camps where the handicapped and people suffering from mental illnesses were crammed while outside normal life went on oblivious to all this, it would not be difficult to grasp the allegorical meaning of this communication in the context of the analysis (it must always be remembered that using the tools of analysis outside the consulting room is a breach of the rules). Such a communication might reveal how the patient, who experiences analysis as something welcoming, from another unconscious point of view, might have begun to picture it as a nightmare, a prison, a place where all his suffering and diseased parts, everything inadequate or "handicapped" have been segregated and tormented, where there is no Red Cross or allied forces to perform these functions.

He may actually realize that these functions will be eliminated so as to allow the "German nation" to function better. This introduces us to the fact that many truths can co-exist inside the consulting room. There is not one single way of seeing, but many: the way of seeing A that fits the way of seeing B that fits the way of seeing C that fits the way of seeing D. And all the vantage points created by these multiple perspectives will gradually become known and, as far as possible, integrated, made to circulate together with the fears that they each bring with them.

The key postulate is, therefore, that communication about external concrete life, when made in the consulting room, assumes a strong sense of unconscious communication with regard to what is happening on the deep emotional level in the session.

THE INVENTION OF THE UNCONSCIOUS

As we have already said, psychoanalysis is a scientific theory of unconscious psychic processes. The title of this chapter was deliberately chosen in order to "enter into dialogue" with Ellenberger's famous *The Discovery of the Unconscious* (Ellenberger, 1970).

So let us start by saying what in our opinion the unconscious is *not*. It is neither animal nor neurological unconsciousness. It is no less invented than discovered. It is not a unified concept; several models of the unconscious are already present in Freud's work. Different models of the unconscious were then worked out by the leading authors of the psychoanalytic approach, such as Klein, Fairbairn, Winnicott, Lacan and Bion. Each time, only a few of the principles of metapsychology are altered, it is clear that the whole idea of the unconscious changes. For analysts the concept of the unconscious is a bit like the concept of time. St. Augustine said that if we ask ourselves what time is, we think we know, but if we have to explain it then we don't know any more. The commonly held belief that it is a unified and well-defined concept is false. The fact is that most analysts work with a concept of the unconscious that on close examination looks more like a kind of mythological animal or a patchwork. This only represents a problem for those who take a scientistic view of psychoanalysis and for those who entertain the illusion that all differences can be erased. It is no problem, however, for people who think that, given the complexity of the subject matter, the various theoretical viewpoints can also be conceived as intuitive, or mythical, perspectives on something that one can only come close to in this way, but never really know in the sense of possess. It is as if these theories were themselves the result of the multiplicity of perspectives on things that the unconscious creates and that acquire a quality of truth and reality, precisely because of this simultaneous multiplicity. That is to say, they offer us a "poetic" rendition of experience that is crucial to fostering a feeling of living a full and authentic life.

So, was the unconscious discovered or invented by Freud? Our position is that Freud discovered and invented it. The unconscious is a concept/metaphor that acts as a kind of probe that both explores and expands the discipline. Only by thinking in these terms can we understand why different concepts of the unconscious can co-exist more or less harmoniously. In Freud's own work alone there are at least two versions. In the first, Freud imagines two distinct places in the mind, the conscious and the unconscious, which are separated by a double frontier (censorship). He also imagines two corresponding modes of functioning of the psyche: the primary process and the secondary process. In the second version the model refers more to processes and less to places, however metaphorical they may have been. Freud conceives the mind as having a tripartite structure consisting of three agencies. These are the ego, the super-ego and the id (corresponding roughly to the conscious, the moral and the instinctual areas of the personality, respectively), although the ego and the super-ego have their roots in the id and thus partially blur into it, as well as drawing energy from it. Many people, even some analysts, have a substantialist view of the unconscious, thinking of it as something inside the skull secreted away in some corner of the brain. They confuse it with the neurological unconscious, and strive (in vain) to base one on the other.

SIGMUND FREUD

Some brief biographical notes. Freud was born on May 6, 1856 in Freiberg (now known as Příbor, a town in the present-day Czech Republic) to Jewish parents, Jakob and Amalia, and died in London in 1939. His middle-class family soon moved from Freiberg to Vienna, at the time the capital of the Habsburg Empire. Freud led the quiet life of a scholar. No particular adventures or exceptional events stood out until the loss of some of the members of his family and his escape to London in 1938 in the face of the Nazis' imminent arrival in Vienna.

By contrast, the events of his intellectual biography are the stuff of a long and compelling novel. The "novel" of Freud's life has been written and rewritten several times. Perhaps few figures in the history of mankind have been the subject of so many studies. First of all, Freud's entire work is a kind of autobiographical novel. Then we also have his correspondence, books written by former patients as well as official and unofficial biographies. These include the rather hagiographic, albeit indispensable, biographies by Ernest Jones in 1953 and, more recently, those by Peter Gay in 1998 and Elisabeth Roudinesco in 2014. Among the books of correspondence are the letters to his fiancée and those to Wilhelm Fliess, a friend who lived in Berlin and with whom Freud shared ideas, research findings and writings, and finally the letters exchanged with Carl Gustav Jung, a Zurich psychiatrist whom Freud at some point in his life had designated as his "crown prince". This third collection of letters need not fear comparison with a novel by some great author. In it, we witness first the encounter and then the clash between two brilliant personalities, ending with their final split. As a novel it is very psychoanalytic and Oedipal in nature, as it tells the story, from the point of view of both Laius and Oedipus, of a filicide and a parricide, which are perhaps both psychologically necessary for a child's growth.

From a very young age Freud felt he was destined to great things. He identified with the figure of Hannibal, was determined to make his way in academia and indeed became a highly cultured neurologist. He graduated in medicine and then went away to learn from the best. At the time, that meant moving to Paris to work with Charcot. Freud attempted to give a scientific explanation to psychic processes. In our time this dream has been revived by the extraordinary progress made in neuroscience: every day we hear of efforts to reduce the psychic to neurology. Freud realized very early on that this was not possible. The two levels are different, albeit interdependent. Psychic things are a set of emerging properties that cannot be reduced to the plane of anatomy and the physiology of the nervous system.

The reason can easily be explained. As we have already pointed out, the human unconscious (the adjective might appear pleonastic, but we use it in order to reiterate that the notion of the unconscious only makes sense in relation to self-awareness) has to do with the world of meaning, language, with sociality. It is not possible to understand the mind except in terms of its social, intersubjective and transindividual origin.

At all events, the text in which Freud tried to explain the psychic through neurology was his *Project for a Scientific Psychology* (1895). As it happened, the book was never published and as such was a failure, yet in other ways it was successful because it was full of insights that Freud utilized to develop his psychoanalytic theory of the mind.

Sometimes the impression is that Freud's achievement is so revolutionary that no one before him had tried to explore the same areas in such depth, but that is not in fact the case. One needs to think only of Pierre Janet, or the philosophy of Schopenhauer or the penetrating insights of Nietzsche, the author Freud refused to read because he felt he was too close on certain points. What is true, however, is that Freud succeeded in bringing together a number of disparate elements in a highly original synthesis: the modified technique of hypnosis, and the subsequent use of dreams, and a device (the setting) which enabled "dreaming" in the session; the technique of dream interpretation and free associations; and, on the side of the analyst, free floating (or evenly suspended) attention.

Freud was also a multifaceted figure. For one, he was a great writer. *The Interpretation of Dreams* is the fascinating story of his self-analysis, and his clinical cases can be read as if they were novels (and indeed in 1930 he was awarded the Goethe Prize, a prestigious literary accolade). As a "philosopher" he revolutionized the way man thinks about himself and he laid the foundations for postmodernism, deconstruction and the so-called "rhetorical turn" or "linguistic turn", that is to say, the consciousness of how the definitions we give to truth on each different occasion are closely linked to the ways in which we formulate such utterances. For this reason, Paul Ricoeur (1965) included Freud, along with Marx and Nietzsche, in his so-called "School of Suspicion". As a psychologist – this goes without saying – he founded the discipline that still gives us the most perceptive keys to understanding the human soul. As a physician he invented a therapeutic device that for some forms of psychic suffering is still the most effective. What is more, in terms of shared, everyday perception, his cultural influence in the broad sense has been enormous.

HYSTERICS SUFFER FROM MEMORIES

Tahar Ben Jelloun's novel *This Blinding Absence of Light* is about the terrible experience of a group of soldiers accused of attempting to kill the king of Morocco. They are kept incarcerated for years in total darkness. Faced with this new, inhuman situation, for the prisoners, even memories of happiness become killer-contents of the mind, in other words, memories, images or thoughts that set off emotions that go so far as to shatter the mind to smithereens, toxic thoughts that trigger dangerous autoimmune reactions. So, a strategy that one of them develops is to recall memories and delete them one by one. Even Borges, in his short story entitled *Funes the Memorious* tells of a man who could not think because he was forced to remember every small detail of his perceptions and sensations. Why then is psychoanalysis memory-work? Let us look briefly at some of the stages of its history.

Freud was a young, brilliant and also ambitious scholar who was looking for a discovery that would establish his reputation. He had studied in Paris under Charcot, who was using hypnosis to treat hysteria, the great illness of the age. Once the patient's resistance was overcome and the trauma brought back to mind, the symptom disappeared. On his return to Vienna, almost by accident, Freud discovered, together with his friend and master Breuer, that one way of overcoming the limits of hypnosis (while still continuing to use it) was to adopt a modified technique, a kind of hypnoid state. It is for this reason that the couch continues to be used even to this day: the point is to diminish sensory stimuli, to induce in the patient a state of wakefulness that enables him to think in a way that is as close as possible to dream thinking and to thus concentrate on his inner life. It's like going to the cinema: unless the lights are dimmed, it's barely possible to see anything on the screen. The reins of vigilant consciousness are loosened and the system of free associations (which is nothing more than a way of enhancing a basic mode of the functioning of thought, namely, that which is expressed in the kind of thinking one engages in when dreaming) makes it possible to penetrate into the most hidden corners of the psyche, where memories of traumas nestle which are expressed in derivative forms in the symptoms of neurosis. These repressed – in other words, unconsciously erased – memories act like foreign bodies, like radioactive zones, like something that is not part of a person's normal psychic tissue. Freud famously said that hysterics suffer from memories.

However, he went even further. He discovered the key role that sexuality plays in the psychic development of the individual and that traumas very often involve sexual abuse. The scandal this caused at the time was huge. We need only think of Vienna at the end of the nineteenth century, where an atmosphere of bourgeois respectability reigned. This was Freud's first theory – which we can call "traumatic" – of the causes of hysteria, and amounts to a "cathartic" theory of therapy. The purpose of the treatment became remembering, so as to rid oneself of the trauma – in much the same way as Aristotle saw the staging of conflicts in tragedy as liberating. And trauma was understood in the real sense of the word, as something that needed to be investigated as a past event, something that had really happened.

This is what the Italian historian from Bologna Carlo Ginzburg called the "circumstantial evidence paradigm" in his splendid book (1986, English 1989), where he compares Freud (who was a voracious reader of Conan Doyle's detective stories) to Sherlock Holmes and Giovanni Morelli, the brilliant art critic who had the amazing ability to attribute paintings correctly and with infallible accuracy by concentrating on the minor details that everyone else overlooks: nails, earlobes, or the shapes of fingers and toes, for example. For Freud, the equivalent was the waste products of the mind, the things that no one before him had ever paid attention to, at least not in the sphere of science: dreams, slips, parapraxes, witty remarks. All these features of the psyche share with the hysterical symptom the fact that they are compromise solutions that allow for the masked expression of impulses coming from the drives (innate sexual and aggressive urges rooted in the body and postulated by Freud as a way of explaining human behaviour) which are seen as unbecoming and unacceptable to the ideal of the ego (an ideal image of the self towards which the individual strives in his search for approval and which thereby feeds his self-esteem and sense of his own value) and to the super-ego (a kind of internal law court that pronounces on what is right and what is wrong), and also represent the expression of the defences adopted to hold them in. At all events, this is the detective-like Freud we have all seen at the cinema, the classic Hitchcockian analyst.

A NEW CONCEPTION OF MEMORY

So what happened then? Freud soon realized that it was not always the case that the memories reported to him by his patients were reliable, even though they appeared to be so. On a personal level, the crisis was dramatic: he had scandalized the society of the time only to realize he was wrong and had to retract everything. This fascinating story can be followed in Freud's letters to Wilhelm Fliess, an intimate friend of his from Berlin and a brilliant otolaryngologist. On December 6, 1896, Freud[1] (p. 287) wrote to him:

> As you know, I am working on the assumption that our psychic mechanism has come into being by a process of stratification: the material present in the form of memory traces being subjected from time to time to a re-arrangement in accordance with fresh circumstances – to a retranscription.

And in a subsequent letter (dated September 21, 1897): "And now I want to confide in you immediately the great secret that has been slowly dawning on me in the last few months. I no longer believe in my *neurotica* [theory of the neuroses]" (Freud, 1986, p. 264).

However, when one thing dies, something else is born. This passage contains the outline of a new theory of memory, a theory which was fairly revolutionary for the time – and which, from a common sense perspective, perhaps remains so to this day. The word that expresses it is the difficult to pronounce German term, *Nachträglichkeit*, translated variously as *posteriorità*, *après-coup*, *deferred action* and *retrospective attribution*. What does it mean? It refers to the fact that our memories are not fixed, but at various levels are constantly subject to some kind of revision.

Everything that is added enters a differential system of signs, akin to the way Saussure conceived the structure of language. For Saussure the connection between words and things is arbitrary, so there are no original terms that correspond directly to things. Every sign makes sense, only within the relationship of identity and difference that is established with all the other signs, as is evidenced by the fact that the same object is designated with different words in different languages.

This is also quite intuitive. A new memory and a new experience throw new light on the memories and experiences of the past. What is more, a new event can give a pathogenic value to something that happened earlier and is now recorded in memory, as if the arrow of time and causality sped backwards. Of course this is not actually the case, because the new memory trace acts on the memory of the past event and not on the event itself. This is certainly true from the point of view of an external observer, but let us try to put ourselves in the position of the subject. Things become much more complicated because the subject does not think of an event of the past as the still living inscription of the past, but as an event that happened, say, years earlier, that was imprinted on his body and with which he has become one. From this point of view, it is as if the past has really changed.

Edelman, the winner of the Nobel Prize for Medicine in 1972 for his studies on the immune system, and the scientist responsible for one of the most accredited models of mind and consciousness, recognizes the part Freud played in this extremely dynamic and innovative conception of memory, and accordingly he dedicated his *Bright Air, Brilliant Fire − On the Matter of the Mind* (Edelman, 1992) to Freud. The metaphor for memory he uses is that of a glacier, which seems immutable and yet is constantly changing.

To return to Freud. The scepticism provoked by his first theory of the causes of hysterical neurosis (a model for the understanding of other neuroses: anxiety, phobic and obsessive neuroses) and his new theory of memory brought him to discover the effectiveness of psychic reality and unconscious phantasy, that is to say, how unconscious representations powerfully determine the lives of individuals, for example, by forcing them to compulsively repeat certain scripts or relational schemes or internal scenes. Of course this does not mean that there are no real, concrete traumas; only that − and this is the extraordinary novelty − it is understood that they can also happen only on the unconscious or imaginary level. Apparently, trivial events can become traumatic because they set up a short circuit with unconscious psychic phantasies, and vice versa, serious events can be tackled without consequences by people with adequate mental resources.

FREUDIAN MODELS OF THE UNCONSCIOUS

The concept of the unconscious helps account for the fact that, as experiments have demonstrated, most of an individual's psychic life is not directly accessible to him. Freud conceived two essential models of the unconscious as a psychic system or organization. In psycho-analytic terminology these are referred to using the terms "first and second topography". In the first topography, the unconscious is seen as made up of two compartments, conscious (C) and unconscious (Unc), that function differently: the former according to the primary process and the latter according to the secondary process.

The primary process uses the type of compositional rhetoric of texts and images that we find in the language of dreams (essentially, this means displacement and condensation, which roughly correspond to the mechanisms of metonymy and metaphor), and for this reason dreams, according to Freud, represent "the royal road" to the unconscious. The secondary process, on the other hand, is at work in conscious life and logical-rational thinking. The unconscious compartment is seen by Freud as a kind of reservoir that hosts not only "phylogenetic" contents inherited from previous generations – termed "original fantasies", the true organizers of childhood sexual experience – but also representations repudiated by consciousness as unacceptable according to currently applicable moral and civil codes. This would in fact be the product of activities by agencies of the psyche that, as in a totalitarian state, have been assigned the task of identifying contents to be censored so as not to endanger the regime in power. The process whereby this censorship unconsciously acts on some fragments of the psychic text is called repression*.

These groups of representations – separated from their corresponding affects by being sent, as it were, into exile – continue to conspire and make their voices heard from the unconscious. Possible outcomes of their "subversive" action may be symptoms of various kinds in which what has been driven out of the door comes back through the window in a disguised fashion and expresses, in symbolic form, the content ousted from consciousness. In the symptom there is thus a compromise formation*, the expression both of a partial acceptance of what has been cancelled and the defence against it. What sets psychic life in motion are the drives, the thrusts that arise from the body and which push towards the satisfaction of the individual's primary needs (sexual and aggressive). Absent from the unconscious are negation, doubt, sense of time and sense of reality: essentially it is the pleasure principle that reigns supreme, understood as the tendency to re-establish in the quickest way possible that which, to differentiate it from the "thought identity" that is characteristic of the secondary process and which remains in its service, Freud called "perceptual identity" or "a perception identical with the image of the object which results from the experience of satisfaction" (Laplanche, Pontalis, 1967, p. 305). The shortest route available is obviously through hallucination, which, however, inevitably clashes with the demands of reality. Laplanche and Pontalis underline that, as opposed to what is emphasized in "irrationalistic" emotional interpretations, "[…] the whole of *Interpretation of Dreams* aim[s] to establish, in the face of 'scientific' prejudices, that the dream obeys laws which constitute a primary mode of functioning of the *logos*" (ibid., p. 306). Thought identity remains at the service of perceptual identity; only, instead of taking the direct path, it makes available an indirect path (for purposes that remain the same).

Phenomena such as psychic conflict, resistance to treatment and the repetition of painful experiences can be explained on the basis of the C/Unc, or rather, Prec-C/Unc dialectic.

If in the first topography the unconscious is seen above all as a place/system, in the second, on the other hand, the word "unconscious" is used more as an adjective to qualify the nature of some functioning of the psyche related to the different "agencies" that constitute it. As we mentioned in Chapter 1, these are ego, super-ego and id. The model of the unconscious becomes much more dynamic and functional. The super-ego corresponds to the introjection of the rules of civilized living as laid down by the parents; the id expresses the needs of the instinctual area of the subject; the ego is responsible for mediation between the thrusts of the one and the thrusts of the other. An important consequence that follows from this tripartite model, as Freud describes it, is that the ego too has its deepest roots in the id and therefore also acts in a secret and inscrutable way.

MELANIE KLEIN

Melanie Klein (whose maiden name was Reizes; Klein was the name of her husband Arthur) was the brilliant continuer of the Freudian investigation of psychic reality, but also a radical and highly original innovator in her own right. Born in 1882 into a Jewish family living in Vienna, she began to study medicine, but then had to break off her studies when she got married and had children. For some twelve years she lived in Budapest, where she was analyzed by Sándor

Ferenczi and trained as an analyst. She then moved to Berlin, where for a few months she underwent a second analysis with Karl Abraham. Eventually, in 1926, she moved permanently to London. Here, she passed away in 1960 after "bringing up" a number of extremely creative students and after some epic struggles with Anna Freud, an exponent of an alternative psychoanalytic current who had brought into being the school of psychoanalysis known as Ego Psychology.

Klein is famous for her pioneering work in the field of child analysis and as the founder of what is known as object relations theory. The main concepts for which she is renowned, and which we have no space to do more than list here, are the following: unconscious phantasy, envy, reparation, splitting and projective identification, paranoid-schizoid position, depressive position, mourning, partial object and total object.

Klein's view of the mind and the unconscious differs from that of Freud in several important respects. In our opinion, the key words to understanding it are *concrete* and *play*.

THE CONCRETENESS OF THE INTERNAL WORLD

The adjective "concrete" helps give an idea of how Klein imagines the functioning of the mind in respect to one essential characteristic: the internal world has a concreteness of its own that is fully equivalent to that of the external world. This virtual space is inhabited by a population of "natives" that we can represent as memories of different phases and modes, relating to the object★, understood above all as a "partial" object. The "stage set" on which the story lines performed by the characters as internal objects come to life is the child's body. Initially, however, this is almost indistinguishable from the mother's body and therefore the set can be said to be the mother's body. Then gradually, as the rudimentary processes of differentiation begin, the set becomes the relationship between parts of the child's body and parts of the mother's body. In these phases the child is unable to have a complete vision of himself and the object and for this reason he experiences himself and the object as fragmented.

Unconscious phantasies are brought to life in this primitive world. Corresponding to every unconscious phantasy is a distinct "play" (in the theatrical sense) and, on account of the primitiveness of the relationships expressed here, what is represented on each stage set is basically a fairy tale world, complete with ogres, fairies, witches and all manner of cruelty.

By way of example, this is the story Klein relates to regarding the therapy of a four-year-old girl called Trude who has been suffering from attacks of *pavor nocturnus* since the age of two:

> Then she came out of the particular corner which she called her room, stole up to me and made all sorts of threats. She would stab me in the throat, throw me into the courtyard, burn me up, or give me to the policeman. She tried to tie my hands and feet, she lifted the sofa cover and said she was making "*po-kaki-kucki*", [kaki = faeces]. [...] It turned out that she was looking into the mother's popo for the kakis, which to her represented children. Another time she wanted to hit me in the stomach and declared that she was taking out the "a'a's" (faeces) and making me poor [...] At that time she had already wished to rob her mother, who was pregnant, of her children, to kill her and to take her place in coitus with the father. These tendencies to hate and aggression were the cause of her fixation to her mother (which at the age of two years was becoming particularly strong), as well as of her feelings of anxiety and guilt.
>
> (Klein, 1927, pp. 28–29)[2]

The sedimentation in memory of these terrible experiences will always tend to be projected outwards and will be the prism through which the subject, once integrated, will look at the world and decipher its meaning. In order to make sense of experience, the subject draws parallels between what he sees on the outside (the unknown) and what he contains within himself (the known) – as this is the only way the subject can know the unknown – and seeks to "force" recognition by trying to modify the former in terms of the latter. At the same time he lets himself be modified by what he sees. Here, we can clearly see at one and the same time a highly advantageous opportunity to know immediately what we are dealing with and the shortcoming of wanting to force new experiences into inappropriate and misleading patterns. The normal dialectic of internal/external exchange is disrupted when anxiety leads to closure towards the outside and an increase in projective activity which is, as it were, "hallucinatory".

PLAYING AS DREAMING

In line with this model of psychic life and the unconscious, Klein does not consider phantasy, dreaming and playing, as the failure of perception caused by a frustrated libido, a failure that may even lead to hallucination; rather she sees the first stages of symbolization – or in other words, the necessary "falsification" of the real – as the result of an elementary transference. The more or less deformed internal objects and the corresponding phantasies imprint their nature on the characters involved in dreaming and playing. Play is a fundamental element in Klein's theory, precisely because her principal focus is on child analysis, and children do not recount dreams but play. She writes:

> The child expresses its phantasies, its wishes and its actual experiences in a symbolic way through play and games. In doing so it makes use of the same archaic and phylogenetic mode of expression, the same language, as it were, we are familiar with in dreams; and we can only fully understand this language if we approach it in the way Freud taught us to approach the language of dreams.
>
> (Klein, 1932, p. 29)[3]

At all events, this is the key postulate of Kleinian psychoanalysis: playing is like dreaming or daydreaming and projecting unconscious phantasies onto the world. It involves getting the most suitable actors among those available outside to perform the stories that recount what is happening, moment by moment, in the internal world. Some are better in good roles (protective inner objects), others in bad roles (persecutory objects). This is what happens in *Hamlet*: by acting out the murder of Gonzago (the interior scene) at the request of the young prince, the players who have arrived at court powerfully develop the story of the spectators watching the performance (the external scene inside the tragedy).

As with dreams in Freud's view, for Klein, children's play also contains a hidden text and a manifest text. Compared to dreams, in play, more importance is given to the process we could see as a kind of editing, which for Freud takes place towards the end to give a certain coherence to dreams, and which he called "secondary processing" (Bléandonu, 1990). Other writers are of the opposite opinion. They see play as an easier means of access to the unconscious than dreams and the "artificial" dream that is free association, because the pre- or transverbal unconscious, a very deep unconscious close to original repression (the first factor that constitutes the unconscious according to Freud, somewhere between phylogenetic inheritance and the first "semiotic" experiences of interaction with the object), is imprinted more forcefully (Kristeva, 2003).

PROTO-SYMBOLIZATION

Through drawing or playing, children give meaning to their experience of the world. Play and dreams help the child ensure that the concrete identification that characterizes the primitive world kept in the memory of its first relations with the object (the mother or whoever takes her place) gradually diminishes, or is rather flanked by psychic representations or symbols. The urge to assimilate the world by transforming it into the terms of one's own self, above all one's bodily self, is the genesis of every transference and every act of symbolization. Playing with the child in a way that lets it feel the pleasure of play means helping it make sense of its experience and acquire tools for thinking. A substantial change takes place in the manner of conceiving dreams that starts with Klein and reaches its consummation in Bion. The dream is no longer a text which has been deformed by censorship and which may contain the fulfilment of infantile desires which have the sole purpose of protecting sleep; rather it becomes the theatre of the mind where meanings are generated in the light of which reality is interpreted.

"DEEP" INTERPRETATIONS

A consequence of this view, whereby the analyst gives children's games or drawings the same status he would the story of a dream brought by an adult patient, is that the dynamic organization of the world of internal objects and the dichotomous emotional logic that governs it calls into question the binary view (phantasy/reality or primary process/secondary process) that is characteristic of Freud. Reality is now conceived as constantly pervaded by the mind's dream. This is why the analyst tends to see everything, whether dream or non-dream, from a transference point of view, and in reference to the

here and now he interprets the patient's every association as unconsciously referring to him.

One characteristic of the way Kleinian analysts work is that they
interpret very frequently, and "in depth", directly expressing the
meaning of the unconscious phantasy active in the here and now
that functions as a key to understanding the relationship and at the
same time as its model. And they do so even more when they find
themselves having to overcome the inhibitions of very young or very
sick children in some way or other. The Kleinian school, more than
any other, puts great emphasis on the role of the transference and the
importance of interpreting it as much as possible. Melanie Klein's
motto is: "Take transference first" (King, Steiner, 1991, p. 635).[4]

By introducing the technique of play, and interpreting it as if it
were a dream text, Klein reformulates the concept of transference,
which becomes an almost immediate phenomenon and not one "to
cultivate" to the point of developing transference neurosis. She rad-
icalizes the oneiric paradigm of the session and places us before the
paradox that the adult's dream must be understood as part of a game
that corresponds exactly to the child's dream. Moreover, not only the
adult's dreams, but also the whole of his discourse, can be seen as a
kind of child's drawing or game – in other words, as dreaming.

The concrete metaphor of play makes it easy to understand the
uninterrupted dream of the session. The patient is now seen as
engaged in the act of dreaming the current emotional experience
in the session.

In contrast to the diachronic perspective that Freud takes on
dreams, Klein has a primarily structural and synchronic view. There
is continual interaction between perception and phantasy, between
conscious and unconscious. As in a Mobius strip, there is seamless
movement from the outside world to internal reality and then back
to material reality.

If the theory of internal objects means a change in interpretative
work with dreams, whereby these are seen as expressions of the transference in the immediacy of experience, nonetheless it is essentially
still transference in the traditional understanding of the term. On the
one hand, Klein introduces a social model of how the internal world
is constituted (the child always stands in relation to the object); on the
other, by placing maximum emphasis on the innatism of unconscious
phantasies, she ultimately empties the internal world of all historicity

and disregards the role of the environment. This is why her theory of mind and dream has been labelled theological. As we know, angels and demons existed before the subject and its individual history.

DEVELOPMENTS OF KLEINIAN THEORY

Examined, as it were, against the light, Kleinian theory already begins to reveal the initial stages of the transition, through the development of the theory of unconscious phantasy, from Freud's dream theory to concepts later introduced by Bion: alpha function, waking dream thought★ and the unconscious as a psychoanalytic function of personality. Thanks also to the role assigned to the object relationship and to the concept of projective identification, there is an initial move away from a unipersonal to an intersubjective psychology. In other words, from a kind of psychology that studies how the patient's mind is organized and how it functions to a psychology in which the analyst is a participant observer and in which, although still at the service of the patient's therapy, the central instrument for understanding is the two-party relationship or the emotional field they create; it is as if the session were a four-handed sonata or a book written by two authors. To use a different image, in one case we have the analyst who, as it were, observes the analysand's mind under the microscope, whereas in the second case both are seen as observers and as objects to be observed, even though the patient is not completely aware of this.

This is where Bion picks up – from the point where Klein stops. For example, he was to make projective identification into a normal, and not only pathological mode of unconscious or non-verbal communication. Also, he accentuated the equivalence between dream (game) and symbol-poiesis to the point of completely turning on its head (as we have already pointed out in the section on the unconscious) the way of looking at dream work★. Dreaming stops being the psychic activity whereby the latent meaning censured by the superego is destroyed or hidden and turns rather into the activity of composing the "poetry" of the mind. Above all, Bion added to the Kleinian theory his radically intersubjective view of the nature of this dreaming-thinking. It matters little whether it occurs at the psychic birth of the mother–infant encounter, or in a concretely dual situation or at the dual/group level which lives in the mind of the single individual. Dreaming and thinking always have to do with a "we".

To take our cue from Nancy (1996), we might say that the singular being is always a plural being.

It may seem strange, but as we look at the things of the world, the force of gravity of our naive realism is so powerful that many analysts continue to misunderstand Freud's lesson and keep to the purely cognitive framework of amateur historicism. It is not surprising then that they are so impervious to the concepts we have been discussing. What is worse, though, is that even when they give the impression of having grasped these concepts, they prove themselves completely incapable of drawing the right logical conclusions on the theoretical and technical level.

DONALD WINNICOTT

After Freud, Donald Winnicott is perhaps the most beloved and most widely appreciated analyst, and has become a point of reference, even for those who are not strict followers of his theories. He is also the most frequently quoted analyst ever. Seven of his works are among the 25 most popular in the PEP archive (Psychoanalytic Electronic Publishing, the most important database of psychoanalytic literature available on the web). Specifically, these are the works on transitional objects, hate in the countertransference, the mother–child relationship, the use of the object, the fear of breakdown, the capacity to be alone and primary emotional development. Three are among the top 15 most cited in scientific publications. What makes Winnicott so central to psychoanalytic thinking? It is not easy to say, but we come close to the truth if we observe that not only did he possess an obvious and extraordinary talent but he also had the good fortune to be working as a scholar at exactly the right time. Winnicott is among the leading figures who were active during that key phase in the history of psychoanalysis marked by the transition from unipersonal to bipersonal psychoanalysis. This period was around the 1960s. Winnicott not only absorbed the spirit of the time – for example, his work is completely in line with Bion's more or less contemporaneous work with groups – but he may also have benefited from being a pediatrician and therefore "obliged" to observe daily how a child's mind grows out of relationships. Indeed, his most famous statement made the point that no child exists unless seen within the special dyad of which the mother also forms a part. This concept is considered revolutionary. Why is this so? Because despite all the possible observations that can be made about an already inevitably "relational" Freud, the fact is that it was Winnicott who brought about an epoch-making change: he paved the way for a psychoanalysis that focuses on the relationship, in which the full person of the analyst, just like the mother for the child, counts much more than had previously been supposed.

Born in Plymouth in 1896, Winnicott spent most of his life in London, where he died in 1971. He held several prestigious administrative positions, notably the presidency of the British Psychoanalytic Society, and published a series of articles and books that are absolutely indispensable for any analyst even today, regardless of whether he or she deals with children or adults. To mention some of his most important books: the essays brought together in *Through Pediatrics to Psycho-Analysis* (1958); *Playing and Reality* (1971); *The Maturational Processes and the Facilitating Environment* (1965); *The Child, the Family and the Outside World* (1964); *Psycho-analytic Explorations* (1989). What is it that makes Winnicott a great author? One is tempted to say that, even more than his originality, it is a question of style. Winnicott has an inimitable style; he writes simple, everyday prose which nonetheless comes up with surprising and "inexhaustible" formulas. What he writes, like lines of poetry, can be read and reread; one can feed on them and yet never have the impression of having grasped their full meaning. His poetically simple writing is thus at one and the same time both insidiously complex and rich, and felicitously unsaturated. An often striking feature is the quietly self-assured way – the fruit of study, experience and sharpness of mind – Winnicott frames problems or solutions as if, for him, everything were perfectly obvious, while the reader is left speechless.

Let us quote a few turns of phrase just to give the reader a taste of his prose. Noteworthy, for example, is the passage where he writes, characteristic of play in adolescence is the fact that the "toys" are "world affairs" (1989, p. 62); or when he speaks of the "flight into the intellectual" and of a "false self living through a mind or intellectual life that has become separated off from the psyche-soma" (ibid., p. 468). Also worth quoting is his review of Marion Milner's *On Not Being Able to Paint* (1950), where he anticipates Meltzer's concept of aesthetic conflict and observes that for the author creativity arises out of the "primary human predicament" facing the infant: "out of the non-identity between what is conceived and what is to be perceived" (ibid., p. 391). What he means here is that to the objective mind of a person observing from the outside, that which is outside a person is never identical with what is inside that individual. But there can be, and must be, for health [...] a meeting place, an overlap, a stage of illusion, intoxication, transfiguration.

(ibid.)

Surely, this is the emotional unison that Bion talks about. The first concept one has of life has to do with the area of "overlap" between the happiness caused by the smiling face of the mother and the child's anxious self-questioning as to her real feelings. Winnicott thus gives theoretical substance to the brilliant insight Keats expressed in his perhaps most famous lines – "Beauty is Truth/Truth Beauty, – that is all/Ye know on earth, and all ye need to know" (Keats, 1819) – and gleans from it a convincing interpretation of the meaning of aesthetic experience:

In the arts this meeting place is pre-eminently found through the medium, that bit of the external world which takes the form of the inner conception. In painting, writing, music, etc., an individual may find islands of peace and so get moments of relief from the primary predicament of healthy human beings.

(Winnicott, 1989, p. 391)

In the sense of harmony and pleasure it arouses, the work of art is a "promise of happiness" (as Stendhal defined beauty), as it offers an opportunity for identification between an experience and the outward form that prompts it. By the analogy with the relationship to the breast, it nourishes faith in the love of the object. If this possibility is precluded and the mother's sphinx-like impenetrability prevails, the consequences can be very serious.

Winnicott adds:

when the mother's behaviour does not in fact correspond to the cathected internal maternal imago, the child does not "experience frustration, unpleasure and anger" ... what happens is that the child tends to lose the capacity to relate to objects. If the capacity to be angry is retained, things are not too bad.

(ibid., p. 472)

Similarly, Winnicott has a surprise in store for us in the review he wrote of the published collection of letters Freud sent to his fiancée, where he candidly asks the question: "Does he turn out to be a human human being?". "These letters provide an answer" is his reply (ibid., p. 474). At the end he says, that, yes, "One could claim that on the evidence of these letters Freud was human, and was a man of deep feeling" (p. 477).

Elsewhere, we find a surprising reversal of the usual idea of interpretation. If the analyst remains silent, it means that the analyst understands what is going on:

> it becomes more and more evident that one of the purposes of interpreting is to establish the limits of the analyst's understanding. The basis for not interpreting and in fact not making any sound at all is the theoretical assumption that the analyst really does know what is going on.
>
> (ibid., p. 85)

In another of his seemingly simple assertions that are in fact astonishing in both form and content, Winnicott maintains that "In natural growth there is a long period in which the infant need not deal with ME and NOT-ME aspects of the thumb. The infant clings to the thumb and also enjoys separation from it" (ibid., pp. 435–436).

In yet another instance, he writes that when the child comes into contact with the breast, he gets "ideas" (1964, p. 46): "perhaps there is something there outside the mouth worth going for" (ibid., p. 47). What is intriguing about this formulation is the word *idea*. We cannot think of this as an idea in the true sense of the word, that is, an idea that comes to someone who can think their own thoughts. It must be a special, rudimentary idea, an idea of the body.

Referring to Melanie Klein he later wrote that if she "had not existed we would have had to have invented her" (Winnicott, 1989, p. 467).

Equally illuminating is his remark about the meaning of music as a container for our most primitive anxieties:

> Belonging to this feeling of helplessness [at birth] is the intolerable nature of experiencing something without any knowledge whatever of when it will end. It is for this reason fundamentally that form in music is so important. Through form, the end is in sight from the beginning.
>
> (Winnicott, 1975, p. 184)[5]

Talking of the creative processes that are expressed in writing he notes that

> as a writer is surprised by the wealth of ideas that turn up when he puts his pen to the paper, so the mother is constantly surprised by she finds in the richness of her minute-to-minute contact with her own baby.
>
> (Winnicott, 1964, p. 25)

As we can see, for the pediatrician Winnicott, the child, or rather the child's relationship with the mother, is absolutely central to thinking about psychoanalysis and constitutes the preferential model for all treatment. For example, this is clear when he writes that for a healthy process of development the child does not just need to be loved but "must also feel real, and if defiance is omitted from the scheme and the child only obeys, or identifies, then the child sooner or later complains of lack of feeling real" (Winnicott, 1989, p. 472).

Insights like this deepen our love for psychoanalysis. Expressed in sentences that are short and to the point, they reflect the calm experience of the writer and chime in with that of the reader. The simplicity of their formulation belies their remarkable content. They are also somewhat mysterious due to the special aura that surrounds certain words: *defiance* and *real* are like vortices that might be the origin of something new. It is not exactly easy to define what the feeling of being "real" entails. While we may think that we already understand the value of "defiance" (one need only think of the pleasure children take in fighting or the significance of tantrums), it is also true that these ideas are formulated in a new and original way. Such expressions are a source of relief because they can act as useful containers for as yet untransformed proto-emotional elements.

Regarding the intimacy experienced in the consulting room, Winnicott believes that the sensory envelope of the setting symbolically represents nothing less than the mother's womb.

In another memorable passage (ibid., 431), he reflects on the fact that "if the mother is lost for too long, the transitional object begins to lose its value as a symbol". Among the various examples he lists is "beating his head against the wall", a well-known pattern of behaviour in extremely deprived young children. It is not easy to understand how this symptom can represent an object that is transitional although "deteriorated". Even if it is a deteriorated transitional object, it still represents something that fuses the multiplicity of mother and child into an indissoluble whole: perhaps this could be the *physical pain* of beating one's head against a wall. This particular case could be a model for masochistic suffering, for a desperate form of pleasure in pain, the equivalent of a phantasy of beatings or a perversion – all situations in which, to paraphrase Freud, one could say that the subject experiences the "high joy" of being present at their own tragedy (Freud, 1920).

These few examples resonate with Winnicott's peculiar voice and through them we can get a sense of the immense contribution he has made to psychoanalysis and the understanding of the human soul. However, to close this section we would like to examine in detail one of his most celebrated essays, indeed arguably the most famous of them all: *Hate in the Countertransference* (Winnicott, 1949).

Its success probably owes a great deal to the choice of a title that has such a forceful impact. When the article came out in 1949 (although it had already been presented in 1947), analysts were familiar with the idea of love in the transference and with (forbidden) love in the countertransference, but they were far more reluctant to include hate among the feelings which they could – and, as Winnicott was to tell us, *should* – feel for their patients.

It takes Winnicott a mere 11 pages to revolutionize countertransference theory, that is to say, the theory of the feelings the analyst experiences in response to the patient's transference. The idea is that, especially when dealing with the most severely ill patients, feelings of hatred and fear must also be part of the analyst's reactions. These are patients who have often been through traumatic situations in their early relationships and have never really learnt to differentiate hate from love. This is obviously then repeated in the therapeutic relationship. Winnicott (1975, p. 195) makes statements like "Should the analyst show love, he will surely at the same moment kill the patient". If an analyst manages to re-discover his split-off feelings of hate, by the end of the treatment he will be able to interpret this to the patient. If this happens – which is not always the case – it is a key moment in the analysis. Why is this so? Because it gives the patient the opportunity to attain an integrated vision of his inner landscape, akin to that which the senses offer us with regard to the objects of external reality: "It seems that he can believe in being loved only after reaching being hated" (ibid., p. 199) (what a stupendous thing to say!). Winnicott insists on using the adjective "objective" and its adverbial form "objectively". And one might think that it is a symptom of the fear of being misunderstood. In reading these pages, some might feel authorized to act out their unconscious sadism towards the patient, mistaking it for "justified" hate. Clearly, this would fall into the category of negative countertransference. In analysis, writes Greenson (1967, pp. 213–214), "rudeness has no place in psychoanalytic therapy […] Aloofness, authoritarianism, coldness, extravagance, complacency, and rigidity do not belong in the analytic situation".

The thesis of the article can be summed up as follows: perceiving our own justified hate prevents us from "killing" the patient. As if this were not enough, however, Winnicott immediately follows this with another twist: he examines the analyst's hatred towards psychotics, extends it to all patients and presents himself as full of hatred, first towards a particular patient and then, in an example that stretches belief, towards a small boy who he had tried to help by taking him in to his own home; then finally, he attributes similar feelings of hatred to new mothers; in other words, he brings them into a situation which we would least expect to understand in these terms and ascribing these feelings to the absolutely least suspicious person imaginable.

The mother hates the child before the child's mind has been sufficiently formed to make him able to hate her. Why is this so? Because in the period when the child is absolutely dependent on the mother, the child is ruthless towards her, what he feels is a "ruthless love". Winnicott follows up with a stunning list of reasons why a mother hates her baby. Once we have read this page, this aversion will seem to us to be the most obvious thing in the world. The baby

> ... is not magically produced. […] The baby is a danger to her body […] The baby is a challenge to preoccupation […] The baby hurts her nipples […] He is ruthless, treats her as scum, an unpaid servant, a slave […] He tries to hurt her, periodically bites her […] having got what he wants he throws her away like orange peel […] He is suspicious, refuses her good food, and makes her doubt herself […] If she fails him at the start she knows he will pay her out for ever […] He excites her but frustrates – she mustn't eat him or trade in sex with him.
>
> (1975, pp. 200–201)

This is a dizzying crescendo. But there is more to come. Winnicott goes on to say that, if the mother who tolerates all this cannot tell the child appropriately that he is hurting her, she must fall back on masochism, adding: "and I think it is this that gives rise to the false theory of a natural masochism in women" (ibid., p. 202). With this last brilliant touch he rids masochism of its association with the death drive★ and biology and returns it to history and psychology.

The child (the patient) cannot develop in an overly "sentimental" environment, and in order to love he must first learn to hate. In order to feel touched by love, he must also feel touched by hate. For this reason he must be able to express his aggression and look back and say: "I was ruthless then" (ibid., p. 265).

But this is not enough. Before concluding the paper, Winnicott once again mentions psychotics, projecting onto them the terrible shadows cast by the extreme passions of the primitive phases of life he has just been describing. The circle closes: psychosis★ has its origin in the failed encounter between the ruthless love of the child and a mother capable of putting up with her own hate. Simultaneously, on the theoretical level, the mother-child relationship emerges from these pages as the truest model of what goes on in analysis.

Lastly, we would like to mention very briefly some of the best-known concepts elaborated by Winnicott for they belong in the toolbox of any analyst: the good-enough mother, holding and handling, the transitional object and transitional space, and the false self.

Regarding the good-enough mother (and by extension also the good-enough analyst), the idea is that being good enough in this field is already an excellent mark. It is important that the mother does not try to idealize her role, that she does not strive to be perfect, as it were. She must know that even her partial failures help her child's growth, she must know how to introduce the world creatively and "in small doses", and to modulate the level of frustration necessary for development. For Winnicott, the mother always instinctively knows the right thing to do. At the birth of the child she enters a state of special receptivity, which he calls "primary maternal concern", a state that can be compared to a kind of normal illness.

Holding and handling have to do with the mother's ability to provide an environment that "supports" the child and allows him to experience a sense of omnipotence that enables him to magically create what he needs at any given moment in a situation of safety and only gradually to be helped out of this situation and taught to accept disappointment.

The transitional object is Linus' security blanket, the handkerchief or scarf the child caresses and jealously guards as if it were his mother and which has the magical power to calm him down. It is thus a powerful factor in the infant's adaptation to the mother's absence and the process of gaining access to the symbolic space – the space in which one thing stands for another that is absent and in this way helps in coping with loss and carrying out the relative work of mourning. The transitional object is described as the child's first not-me possession.

The transitional space corresponds to the use of the transitional object. It is an illusory space that lies between the infant's first sense of omnipotence and his discovery of the limits imposed on him by reality. It is the phase of transition that transports the child from one state to another, from subjective to objective reality. Play, so important for psychic development, belongs to the transitional area. Clearly, throughout life it will also then continue to be the area of creativity, culture and art.

Winnicott observes that, in order to continue to exist, some people who are exposed to trauma at an early age have to develop a kind of mask that causes them to live falsely, while at the same time protecting a hidden core felt to be the most authentic and true expression of themselves. The therapeutic process should help the subject to abandon his false self and become increasingly true and real. The false self lives in a state of complacency and adaptation that is bogus and alienating. Winnicott's emphasis on feeling real and genuine, on vitality and authenticity, is one of the most valuable legacies he has handed down to psychoanalytic thinking and has led to many important developments: a case in point would be the echoes of these concepts we find in the ideas of Thomas H. Ogden, unquestionably one of the very few contemporary authors who deserve credit for the theoretical renewal of psychoanalysis and for its persistent vitality.

JACQUES LACAN

In speaking of Jacques Lacan, undoubtedly the most important and creative French analyst, much the same can be said about Jung. At some point in each of their lives, they elaborated theories that were at variance with mainstream opinion, and likewise, both went on to found their own schools. As a result they were marginalized, not only because not everybody shared their views, or because their treatment practices were at odds with the standards set down by the official organizations, but also because of the originality of their ideas and the way they developed them. The paradox is that while neither Jung nor Lacan are taught in the training programmes of the psychoanalytic institutes that belong to the IPA (the International Psychoanalytic Association founded by Freud in 1910, whose first president was Jung!), their influence is still definitely felt on a more underground level, especially in the case of Lacan. Giving even the briefest account of their theories would obviously be too complex a task and would take up too much space here. Nonetheless, we believe that the conception of the unconscious Lacan developed over his many years of teaching deserves at least a brief mention, since in many respects it seems to us to converge with the theories we subscribe to in our own theoretical and clinical activity, and because it can help clear up some current misunderstandings.

Lacan's story is that of the last great "heretic" of psychoanalysis. Born in Paris in 1901, he lived there until his death in 1981. Lacan trained at the Société Psychanalytique de Paris and was a member of the IPA until he was expelled in 1953, accused of engaging in therapeutic practices that violated the IPA's scientific and ethical canons; essentially he was expelled because he conducted sessions of variable and unpredetermined length. Lacan then founded his own school, which he continued until he closed it shortly before his death. For many years (from the crisis with the IPA until he passed away) he taught in prestigious institutions such as the Sainte-Anne hospital, the École Normale Supérieure, and finally the Paris Law Faculty. Transcriptions of these seminars are available today. Among those who attended them were the likes of Merleau-Ponty, Barthes, Althusser, Foucault, Derrida, etc. Apart from the two volumes of his *Writings* published in 1966, Lacan's teachings were purely oral.

Along with Bion, Lacan is perhaps the analyst who was most influenced by philosophy. This is why his language, which appears to many to be so difficult, cryptic and enigmatic (and for some mystifying), has been better understood in departments of humanities, critical theory and philosophy, than in many psychoanalytic circles. And it is in these milieus that his work has spread widely, and continues to do so. (There are, however, also countless schools that make reference to his name in their title, in a paradoxical situation where unreserved adhesion to the founder's thinking sits alongside considerable fragmentation among the psychoanalytic institutions that take inspiration from it.)

In particular, Lacan came under the influence of Spinoza and of Hegel, primarily through the lessons held in Paris by the Russian exile Alexandre Kojève on the *Phenomenology of the Spirit* (1947), and finally also of Heidegger. Hegel's work centres around the idea of grounding the subject in the I-Other dialectic. His is therefore a radically social theory of the structure of the subject. Another fundamental influence on Lacan was the linguistics of de Saussure, in particular, the ideas of the signifier, the idea of the non-correspondence between words and things and the internal constitution of language based on the principle of a differential dialectic – the Hegelian dialectic brought back to the language system.

Influenced by these important figures, Lacan proclaimed a return to the authenticity of Freud's teaching as against the barbarization represented by the Self Psychology that dominated in North America. He also came to reformulate the concept of the unconscious in a way we regard as extremely interesting, especially in some of its implications.

His basic postulate is that the essence of what makes us human lies in language, and therefore it makes no sense to conceive of the unconscious as a sort of primordial id or as a seething cauldron of the most unspeakable and uncivilized impulses that existed before the child's access to the register of the symbolic, one of the three aspects that, together with the imaginary and the real, constitute the sphere of human experience (more or less corresponding, respectively, to the Freudian concepts of superego, ego and id).

Lacan and his followers have always been very interested in the description of the spool game given in Freud's 1920 work *Beyond the Pleasure Principle* (1920). Freud observes Ernst, his 18-month-old grandson, playing with some toys that he hides under the bed. Then the game becomes more complicated: the child starts throwing a spool and pulling it back with the thread to which it is attached (first emitting a joyous and prolonged "o-o-o" and then an "a-a-a"). In the spool game Lacan sees the process of primary symbolization at work. The child utters a vocable when he throws away the toy, symbolically identified with his mother. According to Sophie, the child's mother and Freud's daughter, who quietly witnesses the scene, the vocable represents a word with a full linguistic meaning: the long o-o-o is *fort* ("away" in German). The reason why an apparently traumatic situation (depriving oneself of one's mother) is repeated time after time is because in this way the child enjoys the pleasure of symbolization: a painful scene is mastered, passivity turns into activity and the child can in some way also take revenge on the object for her absence.

If this is the prototype of symbolization, it is evident that the ignition of the mind is understood in a highly intersubjective sense. The subject comes into being as a result of the mirroring operated by the object. As a mirror image that is sent back to him from the other, he becomes the other, identifies with him/her and can therefore form himself as a subject only if he accepts being, to some extent, alienated by the object. The other thing that acts as a mirror is indeed the object (the concrete person who takes care of the child), but more precisely it is the symbolic system that manifests itself in him and which is deposited in language (indicated in Lacan's writings as the Other with a capital "O"). The unconscious is then conceived as a force field made up of elements (signifiers) constantly on the point of linking together to form chains or of splitting off driven by desires, emotions and fears. The rules governing this continual process of lysis and synthesis are the same as those Freud identified in dreamwork: displacement and condensation, or rather, to use the terminology of linguistics, metonymy and metaphor. In this constant process of construction and deconstruction, reassembling in units that differ from the original units, these elements generate new meanings. In fact, we should say that they give rise not so much to other meanings as to other signifiers, because meaning effects always exceed what in a narrower sense may be called meaning and therefore, we are always faced with new elements (signifiers) to be deciphered in a chain that reaches to infinity. As Tarizzo writes (2009, p.51),

Meaning is not signification. The meaning (of a sentence) certainly includes the signification (of the words), but it is not completely resolved in the signification (of the words). Meaning is something more than signification [...] the signification of a signifier is ... another signifier.

Moreover, metaphor and metonymy, which are the constant warp and weft of language, are

> "meaning effects" [...] It is no longer a question of simple meanings produced by the mutual play between signifiers but of linguistic or rhetorical effects that go beyond the sphere of signification, the sphere of everything that the subject knows it is saying (or is conscious of saying).
>
> (ibid., p.52)

This is why Lacan says that the unconscious is made up of chains of signifiers: not because he excludes their signifieds, but because they are unstable, in continuous generation, determined by the ever-moving play. It would make no sense, as Derrida points out, to suppose that there can be "pure" signifiers. In short, the production of "meaning" is unstoppable as is the "production" of the unconscious – because it is made up of infinite referrals from signifier to signifier. At issue is the meaning that appears and disappears. Here, it is easy to recognize, transposed into language, the game of absence and presence in relation to the mother that the child tries to control. Symbolizing, thinking, speaking are just ways of throwing and reeling in the spool – assuming that the thread of memory holds. The infinite play of the unconscious as a symbolic system of meaning production serves to construct the walkway that saves us from falling into the abyss of non-representation at every instant. The symbol, the word, the very syllable always have, like the spool thrown by Ernst, the significance of an appeal to the object. If the object responds, as Sophie does, "by interpreting" the o-o-o as *fort*, then the absence becomes tolerable. This is why Lacan says that the unconscious is the discourse of the Other, because, by virtue of the constitutively metonymic-metaphorical nature of the word, meaning always eludes the speaker.

The ability of each individual to accept that these new meanings enter the field of consciousness varies considerably and depends on the system of prohibitions internalized in the process of subjectivation.

There are two essential points to be made here: discourses *about* the unconscious and *of* the unconscious make sense for human beings, that is, for living beings endowed with language, and have nothing to do with the so-called neurological unconscious. Obviously there are brain structures that make thought possible, but these are different epistemological levels, which must not be short-circuited between each other. Secondly, as language is by definition transindividual, it can only be acquired in an intersubjective relationship and does not pre-exist that relationship. If, at the very beginning the child, who does not yet have an ego, can only form proto-concepts and not real concepts, it follows that this area of exchanges and the semiotic modalities according to which they take place are essential factors also in analysis and should be the object of an increasingly in-depth theoretical investigation.

WILFRED R. BION

Wilfred Ruprecht Bion was born in Mathura (India) in 1897 and died in Oxford in 1979. Before starting analysis with Klein, Bion already had his own "analytic" history. He had been enormously influenced by his meeting, first with Wilfred Trotter (1953),[6] the author of The *Instincts of the Herd in Peace and War*, mentioned by Freud in his *Group Psychology and the Analysis of the Ego* in 1921, and later with John Rickman. Trotter was a brilliant surgeon who had elaborated a theory of man's social nature; Rickman was his first analyst (after an unhappy, brief early foray into psychotherapy with a therapist he later referred to disparagingly as "Mr Feel it in the Past"). In 1943 Bion and Rickman published a historic article in the journal "The Lancet", entitled *Intra-group Tensions in Therapy: Their Study as the Task of the Group*, which a young Lacan (1947) wrote about in enthusiastic tones. Other experiences of enormous importance in Bion's life were his time as an officer during the First World War and the classical education he received at Oxford, where he took a degree in history before going on to study medicine at University College London. He also found himself working in the same period as Winnicott and was responsible for anticipating the relational turn in psychoanalysis.

The combination of these influences led him to outline a new kind of psychoanalysis that was extremely original, albeit rather difficult, at least on a first approach. At the basis of Bion's research stands the idea, to put it in the words of Husserl, of wanting to return to things themselves, to the phenomenology of psychic facts. His point of departure (and of arrival) was a new conception of the unconscious.

Bion's conception of the unconscious is based on the notion of waking dream thought and on a radically social vision of the birth of the subject. According to Bion, we dream not only at night but also during the day. A set of psychic operations which are unknown to us, which he called the alpha function, continuously transform the raw sensory/emotional stimuli (or beta elements) that we receive from the environment in which we are immersed primarily into visual images (alpha elements). These pictograms, which are absolutely different in each individual, have the characteristic of being stored in the memory and used for dream thoughts and daytime thoughts. For us to stay awake and conscious, and to learn from experience, it is necessary that a whole series of stimuli are first conscious (in the sense of perceived) and then subjected to the work of the alpha function so as to become unconscious. When this process is carried out, the field of consciousness can be occupied by other contents and certain functions can be performed without attention being focused on them. If the alpha function is deficient, beta elements accumulate and a kind of psychic indigestion occurs. In this case, the equivalent to the solution of vomiting would be the development of symptoms of various kinds.

According to this view of the unconscious, the child is born with a rudimentary consciousness. At birth he is "all-conscious", he is subjected to the impulses of external and internal environmental stimuli but he is not self-aware. It can be said that at this point he has only a glimmer of rudimentary consciousness: "This limited consciousness", Bion notes, "is not associated with an unconscious. All impressions of the self are of equal value; all are conscious. The mother's capacity for reverie is the receptor organ for the infant's harvest of self-sensation gained by its conscious[7]" (1962, p. 309).

At birth, therefore, the child has the mother as his unconscious, who is therefore the complement to his rudimentary consciousness. Through reverie, which can be defined as the ability to absorb and transform the infant's anxieties, the mother expresses her love, calms him down and gives him the opportunity to develop his ability to "alphabetize" his feelings based on his experience of care.

In this model, conscious and unconscious are continuous with each other, in the same way that the two faces of the Möbius strip pass seamlessly one into the other. They are separated by a membrane made up of many alpha elements, that is to say, of all the sense fragments that have accumulated in the memory – the "contact-barrier". But this barrier is semi-permeable and dynamic; it is subjected to continual processes of synthesis and lysis. There is no conscious psychic event that does not have its unconscious implication. Conscious and unconscious ultimately become two vertices from which to observe the same psychic phenomenon.

Whether forming ideograms out of alpha elements or creating concepts of things, the same type of process is involved: abstracting or categorizing. Dreaming, like thinking, is an activity of the mind that leads us to forget differences and to retain patterns of relations between things, and to attribute significance to them. In essence, this definition of dreams is a way of re-evaluating the constructive-po(i)etic-aesthetic virtualities of the unconscious.

So, the purpose of dreams is not only to preserve sleep; it is not even the most reliable way to reach the unconscious and does not arise from the differential between the conscious and the unconscious, but rather creates it itself. If Freud saw the unconscious as creating the dream, for Bion the dream creates the unconscious. Dreaming constitutes the central component of the "psychoanalytic function of personality", which operates according to a dual register: un/conscious, in other words, both conscious and unconscious. As Ogden[8] writes (2007, p. 367):

> The conscious and unconscious "minds", for Bion, are not separate entities, but dimensions of a single consciousness. The apparent separateness of the conscious and the unconscious mind is, for Bion (1962), merely an artifact of the vantage point from which we observe and think about human experience. In other words, consciousness and unconsciousness are aspects of a single entity viewed from different vertices.

If the individual acquires this capacity for binocular vision, he can see reality from several emotionally significant points of view, and perhaps this ability is what we call maturity or psychic health. In Bion's thought, the need to know the emotional truth of one's existence plays the role that drives satisfaction, played for Freud. Once the proto-emotions are transformed and made thinkable by the alpha function, they become food for the mind because they provide the subject with their cognitive contribution and motivational drive.

They enhance the ability to perform psychological un/conscious work and therefore to dream ongoing emotional experience.

Between conscious and unconscious experience there is an osmotic, fluid interchange, a continuous reciprocal "visual accommodation". These are tied together by a bond of antagonistic solidarity, the secret of a cooperative understanding, the intuition of a common destiny in the face of stimuli coming from internal and external reality. Viewed from this perspective, the unconscious is neither "behind" nor "below", but rather *inside* the conscious mind. It is not just close by (and/or hidden) but is part of it (Ogden, 2008). As with other dichotomies that organize meaning in classic psychoanalytic theory (Civitarese, 2008, 2011), Bion sets up a dialogue between the binary opposites of primary process/secondary process and pleasure principle/reality principle. The data of neuroscience seems to bear him out: the distinction between primary and secondary process, as Westen (1999), for example, argues, needs to be rethought.

The unconscious is therefore a set of processes of meaning creation that extend along a gradient that runs from the sensorial, pre-lexical and semiotic level of functioning (the only one possible for the "inaccessible" – not repressed or implicit – unconscious) to the symbolic level in the full sense of the term. This is not yet present at birth but develops out of the primary relationship with the object. In everyday life this dream-thinking is always at work trying to snatch from the chaotic flow of stimuli that comes from the real, the greatest number of possible patterns and images to be composed into narratives. Accordingly, in analysis, any reverie (potentially) paves the way to getting in touch with the first stage of this unconscious thought – with the sequences of alpha elements synthesized by the alpha function – and any story can also be considered as a narrative derivative of waking dream thought. Moreover, since patient and analyst constantly communicate on the unconscious, as well as on the conscious, level, there is no event in the analytic field that cannot be seen as co-created by both.

Bion does not create this model of unconscious processes in order to add one more theory to those that already exist but to construct a metatheory. In other words, he is trying to describe how their shared concepts work. The derivations and equivalences between dream work and alpha function are evident, as are the equivalences between unconscious fantasy and projective identification and, respectively, waking dream thought and the intersubjective conception of the birth of the subject. One could perhaps reformulate the Freudian concept of censorship in relation to Bion's concept of container/contained*, and consider it as a special case of a broader mechanism of psychic functioning. The discourse of sexuality in the consulting room – as with any other narrative genre – can be seen from the new vertex of the more or less creative meeting of the minds at work in the session, as a real-time account of the greater or lesser degree of emotional unison (Ferro, 1992). Freud's drive live on in Bion's notions of the H (hate), L (love) and K (knowledge) links, the protomental system, the truth drive, beta elements etc.

However, it can also legitimately be argued that we are dealing here with a paradigm shift, in Kuhn's understanding of the term (1962). Bion does not deny the Freudian concepts, and yet he hardly ever mentions them, if at all. He takes them ambiguously for granted, in a way that ends up silently removing them from the scene, and so we find ourselves speaking a completely different language. While theoretically preserved, they are in fact shattered into a kaleidoscope of new concepts that make it necessary to adopt new points of view. Not only that: due to the subtle play of referrals, identifications and differentiations, by which they are defined and because of the deliberately unsaturated nature that distinguishes them, these concepts force the analyst to exercise doubt constantly and also to take a critical attitude towards every form of dogmatism.

So, not only for Lacan but also for Bion, the unconscious does not exist at birth; it must be absorbed from the mother. It is therefore configured as a psychoanalytic function of the personality that expresses itself in thinking-dreaming, in the ability to give a personal meaning to experience. This is a faculty that is both spontaneous, in terms of innate preconceptions, and acquired, because someone must be there to transmit it to the infant. Now, can we not think of the unconscious as the potentially infinite totality of the language that the subject cannot obviously master? This means that in the very act of speaking – via thousands of unpredictable conscious and unconscious references – he always says something that is in some way different from what he consciously meant to say.

If, as Freud states (using an expression that has become famous), the ego is not master in its own house (that is to say, the individual thinks he has total control over his actions and his thoughts but in actual fact is guided by his unconscious, like a rider who goes where the horse wants to go), now the naive concept of the subject as something closed in on itself has been given the lie for a second time. What we have is not a reversal of the hierarchy within the subject but between the subject and the group. The unconscious coincides with all the infinite meaning effects potentially deposited in language and of which the subject represents only one node, a place of transit where the voices that transcend it resonate. Repression (the psychic mechanism whereby an image or idea that is unacceptable to consciousness is relegated to the unconscious) is subsumed into a broader picture and dynamic which has less to do with the vicissitudes of representations alone and can be better described in terms of the container/contained relationship, that is, within the brilliant and very simple model Bion came up with to explain the psychic process, whereby a given emotional element can be accepted and transformed into thought or thrown away, but at the cost of a certain degree of self-alienation. It is clear that if the unconscious is no longer to be thought of as a maximum security prison where repressed thoughts have to be segregated, but rather as a writing system or an apparatus for symbolization, from the point of view of therapy, what matters is no longer translating the unconscious into the conscious (at most this could simply be a tactical move), but rather making unconscious what initially needs to be thought consciously. It is perhaps for this reason that in *Cogitations* Bion (1992) translates *unbewusst* ("unconscious") as unconscioused ("rendered unconscious"). Moreover, if language is the forum in which we lead our lives and are recognized, and at the same time is also the conceptual grid against which we read off reality, everything that diverges from the normative values expressed by it can be a harbinger of psychic suffering. This is why we can say that the individual has a truth drive, that truth is food for the mind and that if a mind is deprived of truth (understood as the product of a social or consensual view of things), it wastes away and falls ill.

NOTES

1 Freud, S. (1896). Letter from Freud to Fliess, December 6, 1896. *The Complete Letters of Sigmund Freud to Wilhelm Fliess, 1887–1904*, 207–214.
2 Klein, M. (1927). The Psychological Principles of Infant Analysis. *Int. J. Psycho-Anal.*, 8:2–37

3 Klein, M. (1932). The Psycho-Analysis of Children. *Int. Psycho-Anal. Lib.*, 22:1–379. London: The Hogarth Press.

4 King, P. and Steiner, R. (1991). *The Freud–Klein Controversies 1941–45.* New Lib. of Psycho-Anal., 11:1–942. London and New York: Tavistock/ Routledge.

5 Winnicott, D.W. (1975). *Through Paediatrics to Psycho-Analysis.* Int. Psycho-Anal. Lib., 100:1–325. London: The Hogarth Press and the Institute of Psycho-Analysis.

6 Trotter, W. (1953). *Instincts of the Herd in Peace and War, 1916–1919.* London: Oxford University Press.

7 Bion, W.R. (1962). The Psycho-Analytic Study of Thinking. *Int. J. Psycho-Anal.*, 43:306–310.

8 Ogden, T.H. (2007). Reading Harold Searles. *Int. J. Psycho-Anal.*, 88:353–369.

DREAMS AND THE
EMOTIONAL FIELD

In psychoanalysis, dreams play a central role both as "guardians of sleep", as in the definition given by Freud, and because they produce knowledge, or rather they decipher some aspects of the unconscious through a series of operations that represent the phases of formation of the dream itself in reverse. In this first model the analyst's function is to be an interpreter who brings the ego (and consciousness) to the place where the id (the primitive drive) once had been; his job is to remove the veil of repression, especially infantile repression, which, like a blanket of snow, covers traumas, negative experiences, anxieties and primitive defences. In that they are repressed, these elements seek expression by producing symptoms until they are brought to light through the reconstruction of infantile fantasies and of childhood history with all its real and imaginary traumas.

Sexuality, starting from the sexuality of the infant – ever-present, perverse and polymorphous – is the other fundamental element that makes up the logo of psychoanalysis. In the Freudian model, psychic development occurs through predictable evolutionary stages – oral, anal, phallic and genital – each of which has its specific anxieties and defences, and "fixation" within the evolutionary process can form the point of origin of various pathologies.

This way of thinking has changed a great deal over time, but it still remains a testimony to the deepest-seated and longest-standing pillars of Freudian psychoanalytic theory that have sustained much that has since been built. The first major breakthrough after this first model was associated with Melanie Klein, who gave great importance to the earliest mental states, who identified the paranoid-schizoid and the depressive position, and who sought to uncover the deepest unconscious phantasies, true psychic equivalents of the drives. Within this new panorama the analyst had to be able to follow the thread of the various anxieties underlying the patient's story, as well as the defences that had been erected, and also interpret them. Dreams and sexuality (the latter seen in its earliest forms) continued to be cornerstones. New, or rather differently understood, concepts introduced by Klein and the first generation of Kleinians triggered discussions and controversies within the British Psychoanalytic Society, and as a result the Kleinian heritage was subsumed into the body of Freudian theory without any excessive disruption. For a long time a key point of psychoanalytic theory was the Oedipus complex, that is to say, the set of complicated emotions felt by the son or daughter towards his or her parents, which formed the core of the individual's whole subsequent mental organization. In the Kleinian conception, this set of anxieties, anguishes and defences is seen as starting at a very early age. Albeit with different shades of meaning, accepted in whole or in part, the following concepts of Kleinian theory have now become fundamental legacies that belong to all analysts: internal reality is as important as external reality; projective identification is the phantasy that allows the evacuation of very primitive anxieties into the mind of the other; only interpretations of the transference are truly mutative; the death instinct plays an important role, as do primary destructiveness and envy, and so on.

During the time when Klein was active, psychoanalysis expanded across the world by combining with local cultures and giving rise to several different types of psychoanalysis, which many believed would continue to have points in common. A second revolution came with Bion's theories, which, for the first time, placed great importance on the analyst's mental functioning in the session. He gave greater weight to the oneiric element; he introduced a new language as well as concepts such as container, contained, alpha function, beta elements, waking dream thought, continuous oscillation between the schizoid-paranoid and depressive position, whereas Klein emphasized the idea of a linear development whereby the two positions were not readily reversible. Negative capabilities and reverie are other concepts that we owe to Bion and his followers.

On the one hand, the model of the analytic field can be regarded as a development of Bionian psychoanalysis, but on the other, due to the way he re-elaborated it, it can also be seen as an original interpretation. In this sense it has imprinted another radical change on all psychoanalytic thinking, to the point of configuring a new paradigm in psychoanalysis. For this reason the field model was disturbing for some and at first was not particularly beloved, even in Italy. Its most distant roots come from South America through William and Madeleine Baranger, Pichon Rivière, José Bleger, while other no less important inspirations have come from Italy through Francesco Corrao, especially from Milan and Pavia. The particular contribution made by Italy is to have replaced the concept of "person" (the "person" the patient speaks about in the session) with that of "character". From this point of view, then, the whole session comes to be seen as a long dream. If, for example, in a session a patient spoke of a violent older brother who was prone to fits of anger and also of his own depressive attitude, in a model in which the protagonists of the analytic story were people, this would imply the reconstruction of the infantile scene and possible repressed abuses, which dissolve by being brought to consciousness (therapy is knowledge).

On the other hand, in an approach which sees the main characters of the story as belonging to the deep internal world of the patient, the violent brother would refer to the violence of one of his internal objects, while in a view in which the protagonists are characters that make up the analytic scene, the brother would only be a way of allowing hitherto split-off violent and "abusive" aspects to inhabit the analytic field – in other words, the new multi-spatial, multi-temporal structure that comes into being through the meeting between patient and analyst. From this point of view, interpretation loses its centrality and the analyst's function is closer to that of a "film director" who uses different languages and narrative styles to transform the violent character (the brother is the vehicle for bringing violence and abuse onto the stage). The same would apply if at the end of the analysis a patient recounted a dream in which a zoo appears where the only animals are rabbits and chickens. Clearly, this would represent a partial success of the analytic work, since the zoo's sole inhabitants are farm animals and it is no longer a suitable habitat for wild animals.

If this were the same patient with his violent brother, the latter would be split off from the consulting room (like amputating a part of his personality). In other words, it is as if there were room in an operating theatre for a patient with appendicitis but not with peritonitis. The patient's less violent (and suffering) parts may have been treated but the most violent or virulent ones did not get as far as the operating table.

DREAMS AND THE DREAM WORLD

As we have already pointed out, dreams have always occupied a central place in the history of psychoanalysis and in psychoanalysis *tout court*. Once understood as the royal road to the unconscious, in certain models, dreams required (and still require) there to be an act of interpreting/decoding that works backwards on the operations that have formed them, in order to provide them with a passport out of the dungeons of the disguised unconscious and to enable them to convey their latent meaning. The outcome of condensation, displacement, symbolization, and so on, dreams need to be deciphered in terms of their manifest or apparent content if their true, hidden, meaning is to be accessed. This happens using the *passe-partout* that is the patient's mental associations. According to certain models, without these it would not be possible to interpret dreams, and also the things the patient says before and after a dream are considered associations, on a par with the analyst's countertransference and fantasies.

With Klein a modality takes over that assigns value to the symbolization inherent in unconscious bodily fantasies: if, in a dream, a classmate raises his hand, this is a probable reference to an erection; if a patient dreams of a lit fireplace with a row of benches on either side, this might be a reference to the warm embrace of his mother; a patient who dreamt of looking through a peephole and seeing an officer dressed in leather would probably be thinking of a primary scene or the sexual relationship of his parents as seen by the foetus from inside the uterus.

Bion and his followers have introduced ideas so original that they are considered subversive of previous models. First of all, dreaming is not only a night-time phenomenon; at an even earlier stage there is the "waking dream". That is to say, our mind, as long as it is sufficiently functional, transforms (through the so-called alpha function) all external and internal sensoriality into pictograms, or visual images, of which the individual is unaware, and these form the basis of subsequent "waking dream thought" – something like building blocks for thinking. These building blocks are stored in the memory and are then re-dreamt, or "edited", by a "director-like function of the mind", thus producing nocturnal dreams. As these dreams are the richest source of alpha elements, they no longer need to be interpreted, but at most divined; or, if they are interpreted, in the manner of interpreting a poem, that is, without claiming to arrive at a meaning that purports to be absolutely true, exclusive and definitive.

Dreams in the session, enriched by the idea of the "dreaming ensemble" introduced by Jim Grotstein (2007), both in the sense of the set of activities relating to the dream, and in the sense of dreaming shared between analyst and patient, open themselves up to Thomas H. Ogden, the most creative of the analysts alive today, who maintains that the purpose of analysis is to enable the analyst to dream with the patient the dreams that the patient alone had failed to dream and which, as a result, had turned into nightmares (symptoms); or else the analyst's role is to help the patient dream for the first time if he has never really been able to do so before. If they are dreamt, the symptoms can now dissolve, thus allowing the mind to go back to functioning well.

The oneiric in the session includes other elements. 1. Reverie, in other words, the analyst's ability to enter into contact with the pictograms that come to life during the analytic work and that provide constant positioning, in much the same way as a GPS does. In this regard, it is important to underline the profound difference between metaphor, through which we can express something we are aware of (for example, describing a situation of impasse by referring to a becalmed ship), and reverie, which gives access to what is not conscious (for example, visualizing with the mind's eye a ship in a bottle to suggest that the analysis is in a state of stasis). 2. Transformation into dreams: the technique of preceding what the patient says with the phrase "I dreamt that …" is a way of deconcretizing every communication and seeing it as if it were the story of a dream dreamt while asleep. If a patient talks about how his wife is always complaining about the greengrocer selling overripe fruit, introducing the patient's story in the form "I dreamt that my wife was complaining that the greengrocer …" would open the door to a host of unexpected meanings. 3. The transformations into play, in which the text constructed together with the patient is seen as a shared game, which can therefore be likened to a dream. If, for example, a patient recounted that Marco, his violent brother, had soiled everything with poo, internally we would consider that this signals the arrival of a new character, initially still "off-field". We could then refrain from giving interpretations by simply saying: "Welcome, Marco, we've been waiting for you for a long time!" 4. The oneiric transformation of the whole session: if a patient started the session with a question, followed by silence, and then described the fuss Livia, his four-year-old daughter, had made because her father had wanted to rest rather than play with her, we might see what he is saying about the daughter as the dream that follows the analyst's silence and that the patient's infantile parts cannot tolerate.

Naturally, every session can be seen on all these different levels of the mind's dream-like functioning.

If a patient recounted a dream in which her cat, Irina, could not get out of a window because the bars on the protective grating were too close together, it would not be out of place for the analyst to make a comment like: "And there's no way the anger of Achilles son of Peleus could get out through a window as heavily protected as that".

Play, dreams, transformation into dreams, transformation into play are ways of listening that differ from the classic modes; they allow developmental transformations to take place in the session that prompt a process of growth in the patient's capacity for thinking.

THE FIELD EVOLVES

The analytic field is also the locus of all the potential identities of both patient and analyst, although it is not necessarily the case that all potential identities will come to life or be integrated. Sometimes it is appropriate that they remain split off within the field as long as that is useful for the development of the patient's mental life. That is to say, the analyst may realize quite quickly and readily enough that the patient has various Mr Hydes or Mrs Hydes, but he may also realize that inviting them on stage and having them converse with their respective Dr Jekylls is something that has to happen at the right moment. Premature recognition might produce unfortunate effects, something that happens in many stories and films when the main character is confronted with his double.

As Diderot pointed out in *Jacques the Fatalist and his Master*, there are many possible stories that must be "narcotized" to enable the main story, the "child" of the two co-narrators, to come to life and the narrative to develop.

Elsewhere, we talked about how in Bion's metapsychology there are two "loci" of mental creativity. The first is the place where the beta elements (vehicles of all kinds of sensoriality) are transformed through the alpha function into pictograms (the sub-units of waking dream thought). The second is the place where the narrative derivatives of this transformative function of the mind are rendered in an infinite number of genres (in other words, the story that attempts to arrange the pictograms into a narrative). In Simenon's wonderful novel *Les Clients d'Avrenos* the main character, Nouchi, describes how as a child, on her return from school, she would often stand behind a fence and observe her sister, who was a few years older than her, having sex with older men in exchange for some money or a bar of chocolate. The setting was the poor quarters of Vienna in the early twentieth century. Nouchi went on to become an escort, but remained "frigid".

The point of choosing a "neutral" story, an episode taken from a literary work, is because it enables us to carry out an exercise that shows different psychoanalytic models at work.

It is not difficult to imagine where a historical-reconstructive model would take us: traumatic childhood experience, child sexuality, abuse and then cognition of pain.

A model centred on Nouchi's inner world, on the other hand, would take us to eroticized destructiveness and the concept of attacks on linking. A field model might suggest that the infantile part stops in order to observe what is happening in the field, and possibly it is the analyst who "couples" with a more adult part of the patient; this part receives warmth and tenderness, but remains "cold" because everything has happened too prematurely.

But we could also go beyond this mode of analytic listening and open up to a field understood in a different way. One could, that is, think of an evolving field, one that has given up predictability; so no decipherable field is postulated unless at the instant $t\,(0)$ when a certain interpretation imposes itself; an instant that also sees the genesis of an infinite number of possible fields that will come alive and that will be selected by the movement of the multi-group nature of the "couple" that can be known only in *après-coup*.

For too long we have thought that the driving force of analysis is interpretation, but what really matters is time and restraint alternating with presence and intervention.

The initial episode we described could indeed generate any number of possible stories.

This could be the starting point for an exercise with various versions and various developments. Another way is to think of different directors making different films starting from the same basic "treatment" or story line. Creativity lies more in avoiding and preventing developments than in activating specific developments.

In Sicilian dialect, the term "chiacco" refers to a short piece of twine that is secured on iron wires, usually positioned between one balcony and another (either opposite or to the side), where clothes can be hung out to dry. Hanging out something light, a sock or a handkerchief, is a way of detecting the presence or absence of the wind. A patient in analysis explains that if his grandfather wanted to tell whether it was a windy day or not, this is the method he would use. The movement of the things hung out on the "chiacco" acted as a "presage" for the grandfather. In this way he could work out how dangerous the day might be in terms of colds or coughs caused by "movements in the air". It could be either the wind outside or the dreaded draught inside.

This could be seen as a childhood anecdote and as the source of the patient's possible hypochondriac anxieties, or as an active alarm mechanism in the internal world. Or alternatively, if looked at from the zero moment of the field, as the description of an alarm announcing any emotional "draught" that has an effect in the here and now. In this case it would be the description of a field in which the possible difference in potential, temperature and heat might be dangerous because it would activate emotional draughts that are difficult to manage.

IN THIS SENSE EMOTIONS ARE THE WINDS THAT BRING SICKNESS

But if from time t (0) we move towards time t (1) … and then towards n times we have no way to anticipate what kind of field will develop and what narratives will give meaning to the emotional force lines that will come into effect.

In fencing, even in the modern version where hits are adjudged with the aid of electrified jackets and weapons, there is always an initial repertoire of parries, disengagements, moves, feints, double feints, thrusts, "one against", "two against" and so on, but it is the compositional element among them that, for those who know how to observe with an aware eye, makes each meeting a unique, unrepeatable and above all unpredictable experience because it is the result of a combination of infinite variables.

All this is potentially relevant to the development of psychoanalysis, where each change could be experienced as turbulence to be avoided, even if the only way to evolve is to disturb what we already know.

DREAMS IN CLINICAL WORK

Below we describe some clinical vignettes (the illustration of clinical cases) to show how the way we work with dreams has changed in practice, and above all how everything can potentially be understood as a dream made in the waking state, even when, apparently, what we are talking about seems firmly anchored to a model of past or present reality, or of reality present only in the patient's psyche.

MADONNA OR DISCO DANCER?

Marina is a bubbly woman but with certain areas of inhibition (behind which one can catch glimpses of emotional incontinence).

At the end of the session a photograph by Robert Doisneau comes to my mind. It is a shot that shows a line-up of young women, one of whom is bare-breasted, standing before an impresario who is sizing them up in terms of their looks to decide which of them to hire.

The following day Marina recounts a dream:

She is in a country house that belongs to some very wealthy friends and understands that if she wants to escape a band of dangerous individuals she has to give them an "inlaid madonna". Then there is also a girl standing near a podium who can't decide whether to climb on to it or not.

Here my intervention is immediate: "You seem to have decided to hand over the Madonna and keep the disco dancer!"

In actual fact, the disco dancer still remains to be discovered; within her there is at least a small area where she briefly experiences being an "escort".

THE AUCTION

Nearing the end of her analytic path, a patient has the following dream:

She's in America, she's doing well and she's happy with her boyfriend. Then she meets a female psychiatric patient wearing a plaster. The health service can do nothing more for her. So she decides to take care of the woman herself. Then a kind of auction takes place where sofas and armchairs are up for sale; they are not to her taste but others seem to find them interesting. Then she goes back to treating the patient's injury.

It would seem clear that the patient now feels capable of looking after her suffering parts, now that she is in the "New World" that the analysis has enabled her to reach. The analysis has run its course: the "sofa and armchair" may be of interest to other patients, and she willingly lets them take her place.

THE FRACTURE: THE UNDREAMT DREAM

On the day of the first session after the holidays, a patient phones her analyst and explains she has suffered a fracture in the mountains, and consequently will have to wait a month before resuming the therapy. Getting up from bed is unbearably painful for her.

The analyst only has this manifest text to go on, but if he listens to her account as if it were a dream, he will probably realize that for the patient the summer holidays were a "fracture" she will have difficulty recovering from and that getting up off the couch had been a very painful operation.

BACTERIA AND THE POLLUTED SESSION

A patient begins the session by talking about the fact that her dog has an infection in its front paws. The vet thinks this must have been caused by excessive amounts of bacteria present in some micro-wounds in its paws.

At this point I am faced with two possible interpretations: either I can see the bacteria as pollution of the setting (caused by some rather offhand interpretations I might have made), or I can see the micro-wounds as signalling some surplus ingredient and try to restore a more aseptic setting.

I go for the second option. At the end of the session the patient tells me that her dog is better, the therapy has been effective, and apparently "inappropriately" (given that I was not the vet who had treated the dog) she says "thank you". However, the fact is that my listening was geared towards the unconscious dimension of the patient's communication.

DIFFICULT DREAMS: ATTACKS ON THE SETTING OR COMMUNICATION?

Any violation or breach of the setting by the patient has long been simplistically considered an "attack" on the setting itself, motivated by tenacious resistance to treatment, by envy, primary destructiveness, the death drive, etc. All this is designed to avoid the never easy work of understanding that entails the need to adopt different points of view.

For example, Lisa, nearing the conclusion of her analytic path, before the last summer break, hands over a cheque to the analyst made out to herself (!).

It would be easy to invoke the category of attacks on the setting; more complex however, to try to find more specific meanings: the point could be to keep the analyst up in the air and to guarantee his return, but above all it is a way for the patient to express that she now feels ready to take over the function of the analyst and to become her own analyst.

An analysis that communicates "specific" meanings and emotions is very different from a "canteen" analysis with standard fare for everyone. This action, understood as a kind of "mimed" dream, is followed by a dream I had the following night.

My dream:

I have a powerful car that I had not been allowed to drive before, and together with a friend I go to my grandparents' home, perhaps in Via Tripoli. I'm pleased with the car (a Mercedes or possibly a Maserati) and I meet Glen Gabbard [a famous American psychiatrist and psychoanalyst]; we exchange information, I talk to him about a "potential transference", then I go back to my car. At all events there is some new "power" that I can use.

The morning after my dream Lisa tells me about her daughter who is now attending a different school. She wonders whether it was the right decision to send her to this new school. Then she adds that her sister, a prominent psychotherapist, is treating a girl who has a lot of problems and who feels the need to take care of every injured animal she sees. The therapy means a lot to the girl.

I can tell her that while it is true that there is a girl in the story who is needy and in pain, there is also a psychotherapist who is able to take care of her. And maybe her sister is actually the patient herself who has acquired the ability to deal with her pain, so it is time to change her "mistress" and to make the cheque out to herself, as from now on she will be her new therapist.

Within myself I can connect this situation with the dream I had during the night when, in a kind of mirror image, I recognize in myself a "strength" I had not acknowledged before, a strength that allows me to approach, differently, concepts that I had previously seen as true beyond dispute.

THE "DESCENDER" (THE DOWNWARD LIFT)

Simona tells me about a girl she saw in hospital who was waiting for a lung transplant and who seemed to her to be very angry. The doctors were afraid she might become violent, that she might even be a potential murderer.

My response is to ask her if she feels like going down in the "descender" with me.

Perhaps deep down we might find a girl whose lung is removed every Thursday (the day of the session) and who has to wait until Monday (the next session) to have another lung transplanted.

What is more, when the lung is removed, surely it is not unusual to have a fit of anger and want to kill everyone.

This attempt at interpretation sets off a disturbing cascade of associations: her fear of losing her parents and never finding them again, her father being away at work, her being admitted to a pediatric ward alone due to a very severe pertussis that made her turn blue.

In this sequence it is clear how a narrative dreamt by me turned into a range of narratives dreamt by the patient.

On Sunday night I sleep little and badly because of events in my personal life that have been vexing me greatly.

The next day I have two sessions, one with Silvia and one with Simona, which by and large go quite well.

Tuesday comes, and I continue to feel rather sleepy. Silvia recounts the following dreams:

Her dog is sleeping next to her and is whimpering. Then she goes back to her practice carrying a lot of shopping, and her colleague, who is with a patient, tells her that there is a trembling old man in the waiting room she should deal with. She replies that it is not her job, but the man insists that she is the person who should look after him.

Is the man trembling with the cold or with anger? In the session, she also adds that her mother always goes to bed very late at night.

Simona, in her turn, reports two of her father's dreams:

In one someone was due to retire and in the other there was someone who on one level was aggressive and threatening, yet on another was calm and welcoming.

It appears that both patients have realized that my brain is not functioning very well due to my lack of sleep (one of them also adds that she has met a threatening professor).

Seeing my pain and the fact that I was "trembling" with rage, Silvia reacted by "staging" her fear that there was no longer anyone available to take care of her.

Simona used irony by suggesting I should retire and recognizing the dual emotional register (welcoming and enraged) I had found myself deploying – partly unconsciously – in the previous session.

Silvia begins the next session by telling me that she does not understand her brother, someone who takes such a trusting attitude towards the world, who has brought numerous (four) children into it, and that there are some training analysts who only do three sessions.

I ask her: "Why was yesterday's session not a session?" This is followed by a partial self-disclosure on my part in which I talk about not sleeping very much and not being on top form. After a brief silence, the patient talks about waste recycling and how pointless she thinks it is: she maintains that everything that needs to be thrown away should be thrown away altogether, without wasting time separating things into different categories. She then adds a joke in which an analyst puts a carrot on the couch and says, "I too am an expert in 'fields'".

The conversation then goes on, taking in hedgehogs, prickly pears and conkers, in other words animals and fruits that have thorns or spines on the outside but tender pulp inside, and we discuss why these living entities have had to arm themselves with these spines, thorns, etc.

REGURGITATING UNDREAMT DREAMS: PARANOID FUNCTIONING

During phases of paranoid functioning the patient often evacuates his emotions (or proto-emotional states) and then scrutinizes every detail of the environment to see where the emotion-wolf that could bite him might be found.

By doing this, his world shrinks, and he loses sight of the big picture, things as a whole. When looking at a smiling face or a beautiful landscape he obsessively searches only for the clue that reveals the hiding place of the beast that might attack him. Detecting the clue is his way of defending himself from the wolf.

When viewing an enchanting panorama of the Dolomites, the paranoid sees the pinnacle of a mountain top as "the pointed tip of a wolf's tooth" – projected emotion – ready to tear him apart.

This attitude produces spasmodic attention to every small detail and a sense of suspicion. The paranoid patient winces at every micro-signal, at every rustling leaf. Mortal danger lurks everywhere and he finds himself completely helpless in the savannah or the Amazon forest.

Suspicion and the investigative attitude turn him into a secret agent on the lookout for material evidence to nail the potential killer.

It is like a cowboy film, when what seemed to be a hilly landscape turns out on more careful scrutiny to be the "feathers" of savage red Indians or wild emotions that can hurt with their sharp points, and then you find yourself trapped inside a circle of wagon, stationed to prevent expelled emotions from coming back inside the circle (or into circulation).

At any rate, the starting point is the inadequacy of the container of emotional states that have been expelled and now lie hidden: if jealousy appears, Othello is immediately on the scene, if envy, Lady Macbeth materializes, if disillusionment about filial love, then King Lear.

In the case of paranoia, the presence of an archaic superego prevents wolves or buffalo from becoming manifest and means that they have to be masked.

Basically, all defence mechanisms (which, when they become rigid and hypertrophic we call symptoms) are more or less successful attempts to avoid (proto-) emotions that explode or might explode, as happens to the character played by Michael Douglas (1993) in *Falling Down*.

Depending on the functioning of other psychic constellations, one or another symptomatic choice becomes manifest, which I would not consider rigid and irreversible, but mobile and reversible, especially the younger the patient.

Other types of expelled primitive mental states might in other cases turn into bullying: when a herd of expelled buffalo becomes a constant threat that one succumbs to repeatedly.

STORYLINES FOR FUTURE DREAMS AT FIRST SESSIONS

THE ROTTWEILER

Claudia has asked for analysis because she is suffering from an existential malaise, panic attacks and an aggravating obesity that causes her shame and embarrassment.

She works in a group dedicated to "adopting abandoned dogs". She is also strictly vegan. She describes both her father and her first husband as very violent.

The scene that occurs to me is that of a double functioning: on the one side, the "vegan", on the other the "werewolf", the ferocious beast hidden in the folds of obesity and whose ravenous violence is masked by the "bloodless vegan". All the food she eats (especially carbohydrates) seems to have the function of placating the "werewolf".

Claudia is married to a forest ranger whom she describes as a good person who likes meat and who "keeps corpses in the refrigerator" (meaning he is a carnivore).

Thus appears someone who knows how to manage the wolf and its carnivorous voracity.

The dream she brings to the first session is very significant:

She is in a garden where she is attacked by a ferocious Rottweiler and tries to save herself, but her flesh is torn and then people arrive to defend her.

What I had thought of as a werewolf (as I had felt it) is actually a Rottweiler that tears people apart: the vegan strategy of denial and the hyper-negative obesity are confirmed. In the course of further consultation sessions, the central problem is why "the

Rottweiler" is so furious. Had it been abandoned? Were its primary needs not recognized and not satisfied? Of course, there is a reason for its ferociousness. Soon Claudia will start up a "shelter for maltreated molossers". The work continues and the path of analysis is chosen.

MARTINA 2

Martina, an 8-year-old, is brought for a consultation because she has been suffering from very intense and constantly changing tics for several months. She cannot stand thunderstorms or the sound of church bells or doorbells. She also presents a series of slight and changing somatic manifestations. When she plays, she imagines fights between animals and between mechanical devices.

It soon becomes evident that her totally denied internal storms can only be evacuated in tics and mild psychosomatic manifestations.

She tends to distance herself resolutely from conflictual and often violent content or plays games in which she quickly moves away from difficult situations (she wears skates and trainers with wheels to the sessions). It is clear that she is trying to escape from herself, but inexorably the double split that we could call Martina 2 begins to take shape. Martina 2 makes her first appearances in the titles of films she watches on TV: *Jaws*, *The Storm* and *Pacific Heights* (the Italian title translates as *Stranger at the Door*).

THE SINFUL LITTLE GIRL[1]

It is relatively common to come across children with a "double" that can be considered the most likely precipitate of "suspended" potential identities.

Marzia comes for consultation because she stutters. When she is described to me as an *impeccable* (flawless, sinless) child, I immediately ask myself about the "flawed, or sinful, child" I feel must exist somewhere.

She then speaks of shadows that she sees and shadows she doesn't see, but which seem to follow her all the time. I think of a pitbull that starts to materialize without her knowledge.

She then describes moments when she is very scared of dogs she fears might maul her.

In other words, Marzia seems to experience an oscillation between poodle and pitbull, and stuttering becomes the metaphor for the intermittent way in which she holds in or lets go of her emotions.

At this point she begins to be afraid of the devil, and the way she copes with this fear is to rehearse cleaning and exorcism rituals. The fact is that the "sinful little girl" has shown herself and perhaps now it becomes possible to get to know her better. Above all, external presences have become internal and therefore, in some way, already more mentalized and less persecutory.

BELLE DE JOUR

Ludovica, who lost her mother at the age of 13 as the result of a serious illness, was a perfect daughter until she was 15.

For some time she has been feeling "strange presences" around her, and she is actively supported in this feeling by her aunts and uncles, who are attracted by the paranormal and also attend seances.

Everything goes smoothly until the arrival of her first boyfriend, Mattia, a few years older than her, who mixes in criminal circles and is described as aggressive and violent. The "shadows" seem to be summed up and to materialize in "Mattia" (in Italian, the name has echoes of *matto*, *crazy*; is this her crazy part?). "Mattia" would seem to perform an antidepressant function, occupying the place of that which cannot be metabolized, the void of a grief that cannot be worked through. He gives her shoes that make her feel she is much taller, as if she were "three meters above the sky"; she feels loved like a princess.

In her own personal way Ludovica tells the story of a film she has seen recently that unfolds in four parts: in the first part there is a depressed woman who gets her excitement from sado-erotic fantasies; in the second she picks herself up again and goes to work as a prostitute in a brothel; in the third the depression disappears when she meets a violent psychopath who refuses to keep to the "house rules", but has the power to make her feel loved and no longer depressed; then in the fourth − inexorable − act of the film, the psychopath brings pain and suffering to the woman's family.

As was immediately evident, this was the patient's revisitation of the film *Belle de Jour*, suggesting the risk of the serious side effects that can be caused by various types of "antidepressant" behaviour.

SECURITY CHECKS

Lucio recounts a dream.

Together with my friend Matteo I find myself in a small airport without any windows. We are supposed to go through the metal detector but we avoid it by walking round it. We get to where we are supposed to be but a man asks us if we have tickets. We tell him we haven't and so he orders us to go back. I complain but I do as I am told. We find ourselves in a disco. There I catch sight of my girlfriend and tell her that I still have to get the tickets. Some friends offer to help, reassuring us that they will sort out our problem, and they buy tickets for us on the Internet using their cell phones. We go back to the security checkpoint but once again we discover that we have forgotten the tickets. We find ourselves outside the airport, in a small, uninhabited, almost dilapidated village. We enter a travel agent's, a tiny, gloomy shop where we meet a gentleman who tells us that only a few seats are left on the various flights available and that they are all for abroad. I am stunned and start to move away, but Matteo is unconcerned.

We can address this dream in many different ways, seeing it for example as the almost comical representation of a tenacious, moving and painful effort to "fly away" from home, and then looking at the helpful role of the discreet and patient friend, who perhaps is a bit "crazy" because he thinks he can fly, or in other words, detach himself from his home, a place that both reassures and enmeshes.

We can think of Lucio as being afraid he might be "detected" by the "metal detector" and discovered carrying prohibited baggage items.

But we can also regard the dream as the dynamic representation of places in the emotional field of the analysis and its activation of the functions performed by various characters, some as helpers and others as opponents. These functions speak of the quality not of the patient or the analyst, but of their interchangeable roles, which at any given moment lend a different colour to the relationship.

This last mode of listening, which corresponds to the model of the analytic field, has the advantage of immediately immersing the analyst fully in the stories that are told in the consulting room. The advantage is obvious. On the one hand, this way of listening more easily avoids conflating the other's external and internal reality with the invaluable representational device of the setting, and helps us reach the unconscious emotional truth of the relationship; on the other, by being much more involved and feeling in some way responsible for the quality and the endings of the stories being told, the analyst will be better able to understand what is happening both rationally and emotionally.

In the session, I say to my patient that nowadays there are not many destinations where one can go without the fear of attacks or conflicts … and I add (in a rather joking way, letting myself be influenced by the slightly self-deprecating tone that he used when recounting the dream) that maybe very few such places are left – Quebec maybe, or the Engadine. He astounds me by saying that his dream has always been to go to Montana. The reason for this is that when he was a child his father gave him a beautiful book that described how Scrooge McDuck had found gold in Montana (!) and become very rich. "Beautiful! I really liked this story of someone who goes off and makes it on his own", he adds.

Now, the hypothesis to advance here is that in regaining this precious fragment of a happy childhood memory, Lucio is describing the emotional quality of the relationship prompted by the analyst's controlled but playful response. The presence of a father who "gives himself" means that the child can embark on a journey in search of gold, in other words, the opportunity to become himself.

THE INVERTED DREAM AND HALLUCINATIONS

CARLO AND EVACUATION

Carlo is a homosexual patient who for some time has been suffering from both panic attacks and visual and auditory hallucinations.

The "symbols" that I note down as I listen to his story are: ♂♂; ♂ ♀; − α function. These help me summarize the mental functioning the patient is talking to me about: a) contained/contained with no possibility of containment (represented by the symbol ♀); b) the presence of hypercontents (potentially violent contents) with the availability of only one hypocontainer, a situation that occasions his panic attacks; c) an inverted alpha function (this is the reason for the negative sign) that is the source of the hallucinations.

The evacuation of indigestible emotional content seems to be the dominant functioning mechanism at various levels. And furthermore, what would be more functional in the presence of a highly inadequate (♀), or highly occluded (♀) container?

Agglomerations of beta elements can only be evacuated in hallucinations, panic attacks, or in clashes between the two.

Despite all this, however, Carlo has maintained functioning psychic areas capable of dreaming. In one of these dreams *a "quantity of dirty things" oozes out from the wash basin drain and the toilet,* and it seems to be the description of an inversion of psychic functioning (vomiting instead of digesting).

A MENTION OF NOCTURNAL DREAMS

FIRE AND SMOKE

A gifted young analyst describes the case of an architect, likewise, young and gifted, who suffers from a form of "irritation of a nerve cluster" that gives her the sensation of a fire burning inside her.

In an inadvertently comic observation, my colleague describes his patient as smelling greatly of "smoke", and tells me about an intervention he had made in which he suggested to her the image of a volcano simmering and about to spew out lava. He also tells me that after a moment of silence, the patient talked about just remembering a nightmare she had when she was sixteen:

She was sitting quietly in her room when the plants began to come alive and germinate with such speed that they almost stated choking her, trapping her.

It is clear that this dream is also a narrative derivative of the relational moment of its telling, as if to say: "This is what your interpretation arouses in me". In other words, it is as if the architect had transformed the emotions stimulated by the analyst's comments on her initial story into "poetic" images.

THE MASK AND THE FACE: ELISABETTA

Elisabetta is about to finish her master's in philosophy after which she plans to go on to do a Ph.D. At this point, however, she seems to have got stuck. It takes an enormous effort for her to become active in the morning, and she feels assailed and enveloped by depression.

She then says during a session that she is "good at pretending", that she "feels like a smoke mask", adding that her doctorate will also be on the concept of "masks" in Pirandello. One day she lets slip that she is in fact an "anarchist, a lazy bugger, a terrorist". She then recounts a dream in which she *"killed some animals with arrows and then fired flaming arrows at some thatched houses"*. She explains that her master's thesis, which she is finding difficult to write, is on *Il dolce stil novo* and goes on to recite two poems, one by Dante and the other by Petrarca.

My intuition tells me that the "dolce stil novo" masks something else, in other words, the terrorist, the anarchist, the lazy bugger, whom we might dub Cecco Angiolieri[2]. The effect of mentioning this is to throw open the door on the facade or mask of the clever and good girl she had always been (or rather had always pretended to be).

Elisabetta then talks about how her husband plays little songs to their child, who switches off from everything around her and falls under their spell. One day she asks me: "Can I ask you the question again?" I am astonished; I had certainly not fallen asleep, how could I have not heard the question?

The following day the patient talks about subjects ranging from phenomenology to Albertazzi, from the crises of cultures to the problems of southern Italy. Then she talks about the "little songs", emphasizing that what matters is not their content but just the rhythm, the melody, the rhymes.

Only now do I realize what is highlighted in the analytic field: I have "fallen under the spell" of the little songs, which bewitch me and detach me from everything.

I remember a fantasy I had had as I came into my practice that day: I was thinking of Francesca, and I recalled a machine-gun battery on a battleship that shoots bullets up into the sky even before the enemy aircraft have arrived.

I tell her about my observations and she replies with great conviction: "It is true, I am very frightened". It becomes increasingly clear that the wall of words, neutralization, little songs and artillery fire are her most effective means of protecting and defending herself.

There is therefore a time to wait, a time to let the unconscious communication emerge and to form, a constant game of *après-coup* – and then a new unconscious can form.

The song had to be "sung" many times, it had to produce effects, before it took up a position aided by the negative capability that brought it into the unconscious and then led to its emergence.

Another criticism might have to do with the casting of the characters, the need for which is not always understood. The songs are characters in the field called upon when necessary, first to make unconscious and then to bring to consciousness the functioning's that the field takes on.

The concept of enactment is significantly different. Enactment occurs in a dual relationship and always implies a circular movement from past to present to past.

GEROLAMO

Gerolamo is a young boy who has been brought to me for consultation because he refuses to comply with "the rules".

I am told about an extended family that is like a network whose nodes are the great-grandmother, the grandmother, Gerolamo's adoptive father, his mother, numerous aunts, his brother, his natural father and other uncles and brothers-in-law from various parts of the world.

Initially, I am disoriented by the number of people, their multi-ethnicity and their conflicts: it is described how they "throw each other out of the big house where they live". I hear myself saying that "this family is like a kind of circus". Only at this point do I see all these characters as animals in a circus where utter chaos reigns and where it becomes necessary to "respect the rules". The circus is too small for all the animals it contains.

Later, Gerolamo says that the bag is too small for all the wooden letters of the alphabet he loves to play with. Only at this point do I perform a second act of narrative deconstruction and deconcretization. Now I see the story that has been told so far as the description of Gerolamo's inner world or of the field – the circus which we have brought to life and in which each person makes room for a character-emotion that occupies space. We have the jealous aunt, the angry godfather, the disappointed grandmother, the rival cousin, and so on.

So, what seemed like a story of a large extended family becomes the embodiment of a mind – and from another perspective, the embodiment of a field – where we find jealousy, anger, disappointment, rivalry. The emotions are too numerous and too intense. The narrative has become a narrative of his/our emotional field/zoo.

These were the tools I used: narrative deconstruction; narrative deconcretization; re-dreaming; narrative scenography and character casting.

And then there are also the key tools that belong to the sphere of dreaming.

NOTES

1 The title in Italian is *La bambina peccabile*. "Peccabile" is a neologism to express the opposite of "impeccabile" (impeccable).
2 A famous Italian poet of the XIIIth century.

THE TOOLS OF TREATMENT

The first psychoanalytic theory of treatment has its origin in Freud's causalist hypotheses about the nature of neurotic symptoms. We have already mentioned his first steps and touched upon his first theory of hysterical neurosis. Here, we pick up some elements of this theory to highlight how psychoanalysis makes the case for its method of treatment.

FROM HYPNOSIS TO THE COUCH

As we said, in Freud's view hysterics suffer from memories. What does this mean? It means that when they were exposed to traumatic situations, hysterics were forced to banish related memories from their consciousness which they then locked away in the prison of the unconscious. From there, these pathogenic memories act like foreign bodies and continue to exert their influence on a person's life. Like ghosts, they never stop taking their toll in blood. Like zombies, they cannot die. Taking the model of surgery, healing then is brought about by extracting and eliminating (abreacting) the pathogenic memory. Extraction is neither painless nor easy. The patient does not want to remember; he opposes the resurfacing of the repressed memory.

Freud's first technique was borrowed from hypnosis. Faced with the various limitations of this technique, however, Freud invented the so-called "standard treatment", in effect a kind of modified hypnosis. "Look into my eyes" was replaced by "Lie down on the couch and tell me everything that goes through your mind, and forget about modesty and consistency". In this way the conversation inevitably ended up becoming freely associative. Logical links are loosened and the syntax approaches of the language of dreams. And dreams, as we have said, are considered the royal road to the unconscious. For Freud, therefore, treatment is a journey into the patient's unconscious. As in the film *The Cell*, the analyst plunges into the depths of a person's psyche casting about the strange inhabitants living there and with the ultimate aim of "cleaning things up". How does the analyst do this? Basically, he allies himself with the patient who wants to know his own history and the truth about himself, while also fighting against the patient who "resists" out of fear of the truth. Here, the figure of Virgil we learnt about at school can help us take the next step: seeing the unconscious as a true hell. What makes up the memories that patients do not want to remember? Freud thinks they have to do with the seduction inflicted by the father. The prohibition against incest, the only law that seems to be present all over the world, has been violated.

The hysterical symptom presents the sexual act in symbolic form. The symptom is a strange mixture; the technical term for it is a compromise formation. In the symptom two opposing forces are expressed simultaneously: the pleasure principle, which regulates the functioning of the unconscious (the horse), and the reality principle, which guides the ego (the rider). Horse and rider each play their part in the symptom. Neither ever completely wins out over the other. In line with this approach, the clinician acts like an investigator. He searches for small clues that might help him reconstruct the crime scene and unmask the culprit, at which point the case is solved. In psychoanalysis this approach is called "circumstantial", as is the paradigm that underlies it. But what happens when a repressed memory is brought to light? To answer this question, we first need to understand what is meant by repression. By repression we mean an unconscious psychic mechanism that is equivalent in all respects to the more or less violent gesture of removing a disturbing stimulus – as, say, a bee that has come too close and is about to sting us.

Being unconscious, it differs from suppression, which is an equivalent but conscious mechanism. Psychically removing a negative stimulus means erasing images of a scene for which the ego cannot take responsibility and driving it back into the unconscious. The operation consists in detaching the images from the affects related to them. These affects can turn into their opposite, remain floating as free anxiety or link up with other, so to speak, neutral representations. At this point the representations are completely taken away from the control of consciousness. It is obvious that, although it is useful to deploy a device for reordering the psyche, if too much is thrown away, the house of the ego deprives itself of representations that may be useful. Activating this defence mechanism leads to an impoverishment of the person and the unconscious; like mafiosi who continue to issue orders from prison, repressed representations make themselves felt and disturb the flow of the acts of consciousness.

Therefore, when the subject has the opportunity in a safe context to reconnect the effect to the corresponding representation that has been repressed and has become pathogenic, there follows a liberating and reintegrative effect. The individual fills the gaps in his life story, which at this point regains its basic coherence. But above all, he also learns a patient and effective method of reflecting on himself and his experiences.

REPEATING TO REMEMBER

Soon, however, Freud came up against some obstacles, although once again he demonstrated his ability not to give up and to be spurred on by the challenge. After proclaiming to the world that hysterics had been abused by their fathers, he had to change his mind. The disappointment he felt shines through in some famous letters; in one of these, for example, he expresses his bitterness at no longer believing his patients. The veracity of the memories of the traumas underwent a crisis. Freud then shifted the focus of his attention from material and historical reality to psychic reality. There had to be a reason if some pseudo-memories established themselves as true memories. The reason lay in the power exerted by certain unconscious and universal fantasies, namely, the fantasies of incest and parricide as described in works of great literature such as Sophocles' *Oedipus Rex*, Shakespeare's *Hamlet* or Dostoevsky's *The Brothers Karamazov*.

The fact that a psychic reality exists means that we are inhabitants of two worlds, the world of our senses and the world of our psychic life, and both demand a toll from us if we want to lead undisturbed daily lives. If fantasies belong to the whole of mankind and to all individuals, it is also, however, to be assumed that in certain specific situations, which mostly have to do with children's early relations with their parents, something has "activated" these fantasies beyond measure, making them pathogenic. This may have been an excess of closeness to, or distance from, the most important parental figures, and as a result the introjection of an analogous function of distance regulation in emotional relationships has failed: either too close, making for an "incestuous" object, or too distant, and therefore pro-ducing an irresponsible object.

This is where the traditional tendency of psychoanalysis to reconstruct the patient's biography, leaning towards history as it was, begins to lose ground, precisely because the pathogenic nucleus must have been created by the interweaving of the external and the internal world. History is relativized and its role is reduced. Also, in therapy, historical investigation makes way for the collaborative exploration of the unconscious life of the analysand – or rather, of the couple.

If the case of Dora marks the high point of the circumstantial method, in order to witness the key shift in method we need to turn to the case of the Wolf-Man. Initially, Freud engaged in assiduous historical research but then gave up, turned instead to fantasy and pronouncing his dry *non-liquet* (it does not matter) about the basis in reality of the Wolf-Man's famous dream. This is the account of the dream, undoubtedly among the most famous in the history of psychoanalysis.

> *I dreamt that it was night and that I was lying in my bed. (My bed stood with its foot towards the window; in front of the window there was a row of old walnut trees. I know it was winter when I had the dream, and night-time.) Suddenly the window opened of its own accord, and I was terrified to see that some white wolves were sitting on the big walnut tree in front of the window. There were six or seven of them. The wolves were quite white, and looked more like foxes or sheep-dogs, for they had big tails like foxes and they had their ears pricked like dogs when they pay attention to something. In great terror, evidently of being eaten up by the wolves, I screamed* and woke up. My

nurse hurried to my bed, to see what had happened to me. It took quite a long while before I was convinced that it had only been a dream; I had had such a clear and life-like picture of the window opening and the wolves sitting on the tree. At last I grew quieter, felt as though I had escaped from some danger, and went to sleep again.

The only piece of action in the dream was the opening of the window; for the wolves sat quite still and without making any movement on the branches of the tree, to the right and left of the trunk, and looked at me. It seemed as though they had riveted their whole attention upon me. – I think this was my first anxiety-dream.

(Freud, 1914c, 29)

Freud tries in every way possible to reconstruct a real event of trau-matic significance (a sexual scene between the parents), which the child, four years old at the time of the dream, would have witnessed at the age of one and a half, but in the end he gives up and ultimately concedes that what matters is the fantasy. In the same text he devel-ops what has now become the very topical conception of memory functioning, as confirmed decades later by neuroscience data. There are no such things as fixed memories, but rather mnestic traces that are continually being reworked and updated. It's like the language system. Each term takes on meaning as part of the system, based on the game of identity and difference with all other terms, and each new term added to the system potentially changes all the others. Freud uses this notion, which can be extended to the physiological functioning of memory, to construct a two-stage theory of trauma. Innocent scenes can have a pathogenic effect only after the sexual maturation that occurs in puberty.

As we see, from the very beginning, psychoanalysis has been a science of memory.

But then if the analyst can no longer trust memories, and if it is also true that there are memories that remain inaccessible, how can he treat his patient? To solve this problem Freud elaborates the the-ory of "transference", a term that, like many other psychoanalytic expressions, has even entered everyday language. The problem of the unreliability of memories can be avoided. In Dora, Freud notes that fingertips speak when language is silent. The patient remembers in the same way as he expresses previously learned patterns in significant relationships. Repeating is indeed a way of remembering. The patient thus "transfers" the experiences linked to his parents on to the analyst, in so far as he has become an important figure on whom he depends for his well-being. The analyst works like a reagent that activates certain processes, which he can then study in detail. At this point he has knowledge that is no longer only the result of an abstract understanding of the unconscious mechanisms of psychic life but also of experiments carried out in the special laboratory that is the analytic setting (in other words, the set of rules regarding time, place and money that regulate the sessions), and is able to transmit them to the patient.

In the concept of transference neurosis the focus is on an essential aspect of psychoanalysis, present in various ways in all its models, namely the idea that the understanding and care that define the subject's truth about himself must necessarily involve an intense and prolonged experience. Only a new meaningful relationship can be truly transformative. The new experience gives access to understanding that is integrated, rational and affective.

THE TRUTH DRIVE

There is an important point to make here: for Freud it was clear from the beginning that analysis stood in close relationship to the truth: the patient is treated by being acquainted with the truth about himself. Often, this truth is seen as dependent on the undisputed authority of the analyst. However, by purposely nurturing a new neurosis, which is "extracted" or derived from the patient's childhood neurosis, an experimental neurosis in which the analyst is involved (termed transference neurosis), the analyst seeks to obtain evidence that is based on a shared experience. His aim is to use what happens before the eyes of both parties to reinforce the incontrovertible strength of his interpretations. Herein lie the roots of a principle of truth-as-immediacy and the idea of unison (intersubjective agreement or consensuality).

Truth is a strategic element of treatment and the lens used to focus on it is the relationship that becomes established between analyst and patient. This relationship is at one and the same time old, because it repeats old patterns, and new, because the analyst refrains from identifying with the complementary role. Or at least so he believes. The fact is that there is no guarantee this will happen. The analyst too has an unconscious and although he is trained to scrutinize and interpret it, clearly he cannot help becoming involved consciously and especially unconsciously in complex interrelational games. In this first phase of the development of the concept, transference is seen above all in terms of misunderstanding (Freud calls it a "false connection", a *mésalliance*, Freud, 1892–5, p. 303). Blinded by his own declarative and embodied memories, by a complex system of expectations and already preconceived solutions for conflicts, the patient will systematically tend to "make mistakes" in the way he addresses the analyst. The interpretation of transference, the analyst's prime instrument of treatment, just as the scalpel is for the surgeon, will equally, systematically, correct the error. The patient is wrong because he navigates the world using cognitive and emotional maps that are now obsolete.

After transference, Freud then went on to "discover" countertransference. The experiential and affective dimension that analysis increasingly takes on also extends to the analyst. He cannot remain imperturbable and neutral. He will react to the patient with his *own* transference and with his responses to the patient's transference. The doctor cannot avoid having feelings towards the patient. Since then the analysis of transference and countertransference has been the alpha and omega of classical treatment and also of various other models that deviate from it in some important respects.

Even in the Kleinian model, interpretation is the main tool of treatment, perhaps even more so given the way it is used, since it is no longer aimed at transference but rather at explicating the unconscious phantasy active at that moment in the patient. As in classical psychoanalysis, the question of the more or less undisputed authority of the analyst remains. As we know, this is precisely the point that other psychoanalytic models, for example relational models, have sharply criticized. Let us now examine this aspect in more detail, as it is that which is most closely related to the question of truth in psychoanalysis. As we have seen, for Freud, analysis is a struggle in which the analyst must overcome the patient's resistance to knowledge. For him the primary idea remains that the patient misunderstands and distorts the truth of the emotional experience he is going through. There is a risk the analyst might impose on the patient his own truth for pedagogical-educational reasons and Freud himself had an early and dramatic experience of this in his "neurotica" crisis. The patient is certainly not seen as the analyst's "best colleague", as the person who "treats" his therapist, if necessary, and continually signals to him his mode of operation through derivatives of unconscious thought.

The same is true, and perhaps even more so, with regard to Klein-ian interpretations. Since there will always be an unconscious part of the patient's mind that welcomes them, other parameters are set aside in order to see the effect they produce. Deep, intrepid, obliv-ious to how much the patient can tolerate and to the psychic pain they might provoke, aimed at the unconscious (which is supposed to "automatically" recognize their goodness) – this is how one might describe Kleinian interpretations. The analyst is pictured as being "naturally" capable of "understanding" what happens in the transfer-ence relationship. But how do we know whether an interpretation is firmly founded on the material available and what criterion of truth underlies this conviction?

It is easy to see that Klein started from the point where Freud stopped, from the discovery of psychic reality, and clearly she gave this concept a previously lacking vivacity and richness of meaning. Psychic life is no longer seen as the Freudian scene dominated by the main psychic agencies – ego, super-ego and id – but as a crowded theatre of objects (unconscious fantasies) expressing multiple forms of relationships with objects. Everything becomes more alive, kalei-doscopic and "scary". The shadows of this theatre are continually projected onto the individual's conscious life and exert a powerful influence. It is as if the analyst were saying through his interpreta-tion: look, now you see Candide, now Macbeth, now the Mistress of the Inn, now Batman, now Linus … Obviously, in this theatre he recognizes himself as an actor. Since the most powerful fantasies are the most archaic, for the most part it will be a world of horror films or fairy tales. Klein's brilliant attempts to describe it betray a typical touch of cruelty.

Let us return to our parameters of immediacy (or immanence) and unison as components of the thread that runs through the whole of psychoanalysis. Immediacy is extolled to the maximum level: by definition, Kleinian analysis, which grew out of the treatment of chil-dren and the technique of play, addresses the here and now; the sec-ond component pales a little compared to Freud, because little care is taken of how the patient accepts the interpretation. With children, dreams become play. Playing is like dreaming. Playing means creating meaningful plots for the available characters and for the emotions we attribute to them. Another important tool in the Kleinian "instru-mentarium" is the concept of projective identification. This expression refers to the act of discarding unwanted content and depositing it in the other. We can see how Klein is already starting to make psychoanalysis more "relational". Repression is replaced by splitting, and the unconscious is replaced by the other, or rather by an unconscious that is already postulated differently, less as a psychic place within the individual and more as a symbolic system that cannot be dominated by the ego and is intrinsically social in nature.

Melanie Klein died in 1960. In the period from the early 1960s until the mid-1970s psychoanalysis underwent a profound renewal. This period saw the publication of books by Winnicott, Bion and Kohut. The transition began from a psychoanalysis that was unipersonal (centred on the isolated subject) to a bipersonal or "group" psychoanalysis. The positivist paradigm went through a crisis and psychoanalysis necessarily felt the repercussions. The work of these authors bore a strong relational imprint. The motto could be borrowed from Winnicott, who wrote that the child does not exist: it does not exist unless it is seen as a member of a dyad that also includes the mother. At least two important consequences flow from this idea. The relationship between mother and child becomes the model of how a mind can only be born and develop from another mind; secondly, it also becomes the model of therapeutic action. Helping a mind grow is different from fighting an enemy who refuses to know the truth of the unconscious. Furthermore, the analyst also has an unconscious and must now necessarily take it into proper account. In Winnicott, treatment becomes the way to promote the process of *personalization*, of becoming a person (as Winnicott defines the term he himself introduced), of instituting a mind in the body (without ever losing the body's mind) and a way of attaining a feeling of being alive, real and authentic. Illness is seen as a defence adopted to protect a fragile and hidden self that has been rejected by the world. The analyst-as-mother must have psychic qualities that are not theorized as they are in Kleinian psychoanalysis.

Bion, who was in analysis with Klein, developed the model on an even more profound level than the "pediatrician" Winnicott. The problem arose of elaborating a theory of psychoanalytic observation that could bring psychoanalysis to a higher level of formalization. To repeat: for this reason he started again "from things themselves". In his view the analyst's most important tool is his particular receptivity to the patient's anxieties and his ability to receive and transform them, similar to the mother's ability to sense what her child needs and to do what is necessary to calm him. This action of containment and transformation equates to giving an entire, full, affective and rational meaning to what is going on. The child and the patient gradually acquire the method needed to carry out the same operation by themselves. Understanding and accepting the patient's anxieties means experiencing a moment of encounter, unison, reflection, being "at one".

There are various expressions that convey more or less the same idea. Emotional unison creates a sort of proto-concept (not a real concept), an initial intersubjective agreement that underlies what is then held to be true within a given community. Every happy experience of sense, even before significance, constructs the mind. Pieces of significance (when they belong to the semantic order of language), or bits of sense (when they belong to the semiotic order of bodily schemas, even so learned) are like Lego bricks that can fit into each other to form wonderful structures. The analyst helps the patient draw the most effective cognitive/affective maps to negotiate the world. At first impact with the real, proto-emotions and proto-sensations are generated that must be transformed into memories, images endowed with meaning and thoughts. Beta elements must be admitted to the realm of symbol and language. There are two sides to the dream, one that conceals the truth and one that generates it poetically, and Bion emphasizes the latter. Thinking comes to be equated with dreaming or with unconscious thought and becomes a psychoanalytic function of personality.

The problem of differentiating between dream-thinking (that which is produced by what Freud refers to as the primary process) and logical-rational thinking (secondary process) does of course remain. In this regard, we believe that we should not think of a clear caesura; the two modes of thinking should be represented as arranged along a continuum. It would, hypothetically, be up to the function of attention, the ability that human beings have to focus intentionally on the smallest details of the field of consciousness, to explain how one or another mode can be activated. For Vygotsky and Lurija (1984) the prime function of language is not to communicate, but to act as a means of monitoring attention. In fact, they make a distinction between natural attention, the type that responds to stimulus, and what they call "artificial" attention, which responds to language.

EMOTIONAL UNISON

Now we come to the post-Bionian model of the analytic field. This is the model that, in the most radical and rigorous way, sets aside the patient's history and material reality in order to focus on the profound emotional experience in the present moment of the meeting between patient and analyst. It is like a kind of physiotherapy or gymnastics for the mind. The analyst listens to whatever is said, both what the patient says and what he himself says, as if it were a narrative derivative of their shared unconscious thought (although it could be said that in general it is not the subject but the group that thinks: what would otherwise be the point of saying that we are "spoken by the unconscious"?). He thus uses a radical criterion of immanence; he pays attention to what is present and alive in the here and now. What is more, he takes utmost responsibility for his own subjectivity. The patient brings his often bleeding wounds to the analysis. The important thing then is to staunch the patient's wound and not to explain how coagulation works.

The analyst listens to all of the patient's verbal and non-verbal communications and to its own internal speech, whether explicit or not, verbal and non-verbal, as if the couple were engaged in a common effort to make sense of the experience. Obviously, the analysis offers help and support; where necessary it reassures and guides. During a prolonged relationship it is obvious that in one way or another the gold of interpretation – interpretation that centres on the you-and-I works at 250 volts, but normal bulbs do not take more than 220 volts! – whether saturated or unsaturated, explicit or implicit, will be mixed with other metals, less noble but no less important. It would be pointless to invoke the idea of a sort of purity of analytic intervention; precisely the centrality of the semiotic component blurs the distinction between suggestion and interpretation.

We have been looking at some of the tools in the analyst's toolkit: unconscious, transference, countertransference, unconscious fantasy, projective identification, unison, reverie, interpretation, field. But what do analyst and patient actually do? After some preliminary meetings (usually between two and four), they may find that there are valid reasons to undertake therapy, and so they decide to meet for a relatively lengthy period of time (on average from one to three years in the case of psychotherapy, or from four to five in the case of analysis), and with a sufficient number of sessions to carry out the work they have set out to do. Classical treatment takes place with a frequency of three to five weekly sessions, each lasting 45–50 minutes. As already mentioned, nowadays, there tends to be more flexibility on these points. Typical treatment is often an aim rather than an essential starting point. There are many factors that explain this change – economic, physical and psychological, cultural and practical factors (the nomadic nature of many modern professions). However, more is involved: a theoretical change has also taken place. At all events, once the time and place of the sessions have been decided, the patient "hires" portions of the analyst's time, and he pays a fee, even if he does not use that time. There are various reasons for this, but the essential one is that we need to protect the "theatrical" space of the analysis from the conscious and unconscious manipulations of the actors involved, both of whom could "set it on fire".

This means that if a patient decides not to go to the session on a particular day, he or she must feel free to do so, and without having to endure an overwhelming sense of guilt, knowing that this could also be analyzed. The analyst informs the patient about the so-called "fundamental rule", that is, he asks him to act as if he were a traveller in a train compartment describing the landscape that flows past the window – in this case, the thoughts, images and sensations that arise in his consciousness – without worrying about saying anything unseemly or that may sound trivial or offensive. The analyst has a benevolent and participatory, non-judgmental attitude. Today, many analysts prefer to tell the patient that he has a space where he can talk about what he wants, say what he wants – or equally, be silent – and that the analyst will do the same. This avoids issuing paradoxical injunctions along the lines of: "be spontaneous!". The reason for trying to loosen the logical links of discourse is, as we have said, to come closer to a kind of speaking-as-dreaming. One succinct way of describing dream language is to say that it is akin to poetry. The musical or semiotic discourse overrides the logical-rational framework, where the emphasis is on semantics and content. Metaphor and metonymy reign supreme – the two rhetorical figures Lacan equated with displacement and condensation, the two main mechanisms highlighted by Freud together with the representations and secondary elaboration that are at work in the way in which the mind creates the images of the dream (dream-work or *Traumarbeit*). As with poetry, expressions in dream language are characteristically ambiguous.

On the one hand, they provide a way of coming quickly into contact with the contents of a person's inner life; on the other, they lend themselves wonderfully to explorative and projective work.

In the past (although it is true that many analysts still work this way on patients' dreams) the analyst would investigate the manifest content and then work back to latent thoughts that are hidden by the dreamer because they are incompatible with the psychic agency of the super-ego, which Freud saw as a kind of internal tribunal. The more recent relational or intersubjective approach prefers to work *with* the patient's dreams. We are not so much looking for hidden contents – although, if it comes to it, even these can be involved (the old philosophical precept of "know yourself" has not been entirely abolished) – but rather we engage in a sort of joint effort to make sense of the images that occur in the dream and to integrate them into the patient's story, the reality of his life using the litmus test of the therapeutic relationship.

Typically, the dream "constrains" us to adopt varying perspectives on reality, all simultaneously valid, similar to what we do when we read poetry. If we consider that this work with dreams is rooted in the emotional terrain shared by the analytic couple and not only in abstract thought, we understand that it coincides with the growth of the mind and with a feeling of truth and reality. This is why we say that we have now moved on, or are attempting to move on, towards an "aesthetic" paradigm – certainly not in the usual sense of aesthetic as precious and over-refined, but in the sense of full, integrated and somatopsychic. The individual is constituted in a primarily inter-subjective and sensorial dimension (*aísthesis* means "sensation"). To borrow the title of a book by Giampaolo Lai (1985), ideally we engage in a "happy conversation". "Happy" here means being on the same wavelength and is not necessarily connected to positive or pleasant topics. Often, in fact, the opposite is the case. The "pleasure" lies in feeling understood, reflected, accepted, contained. Speaking-as-dreaming is of course a kind of ideal state which one can sometimes come close to – and sometimes not. There can be very painful phases in therapy, marked by silence or insignificance, hatred or frustration. The theories of psychoanalysis place the analyst in a position where more often than not he is able to tolerate situations which give one the feeling that the arrow of time has stopped. Over time the relationship between analyst and patient intensifies and, when things go well, it becomes a new and profound life experience.

If the experience is "happy" or "good", the subject restructures his self, internalizes new patterns of interaction that are not only intellectual but also "procedural" (to use the adjective that refers to the type of memory that allows us to do things "without really thinking": to ski, to play the piano and to tap out words on a computer keyboard). The relationship is no longer (and not just) an "artificial" relationship – hence the idea that the transference disappears at the end of treatment – but is a genuine encounter between two people who are interested in telling each other directly and indirectly (allegorically) the "sentimental" story of their meeting, and who get pleasure and profit from doing so. It is no longer (and not just) a process that provides a series of stations to pass through or issues to tackle, but an exploratory journey whose ending reveals itself only gradually.

TRANSFERENCE LOVE AND DEPENDENCE

People often talk about the fear of becoming dependent on therapy and on the figure of the therapist. If things are conducted according to the principles of science and conscience, this fear is unfounded. There is no difference between this dependence and the dependence felt towards any other health care provider; it is functional to the work to be done, even if, in the case of analysis, it can take on singular forms, for example, the so-called transference love. Numerous Hollywood films have perpetuated the stereotype of the patient who falls in love with the analyst. The traditional idea of transference love is, so to speak, love as in a comedy of errors. The patient falls in love with the therapist because unconsciously she sees in him the father who is the object of her incestuous desires. Initially Freud talked about transference love as "the fire in the theatre". Indeed, Breuer, who some see as the inventor of psychoanalysis, fled from Anna O. when she suddenly threw her arms around his neck. Freud himself admitted that he had come very close on several occasions. Then, however, he turned it into the driving force of the treatment itself. In some ways this is self-evident: if the temperature of the relationship rises, it is easier for the iron of the neurosis to work and bend. The treatment has greater transformative potential. Besides, it would be absurd to think of something so totally artificial. Freud's position on love is ambiguous. On the one hand, he sees it as a delusion and a denial of reality; on the other, he regards it as the expression of a powerful desire to learn, an openness to reality and to a true, profound knowledge of the other. This uncertainty is reflected in the suspicion of classical psychoanalysis towards transference love, seen as "false" compared to its more genuine or "true" version. Equally vague and insufficiently defined are the principles of translating the unconscious into conscious and bringing the id under the control of the ego. The value of truth is intrinsic to emotional unison, in the same way as, in Freud's terms, a deep knowledge of the object is intrinsic to love for that person. The one thing that is certain is that transference love is explosive material. When it is not treated properly, it can be the cause of destructive transgression.

The fact is that several authors have emphasized the meaning of love/sentiment in treatment. Talking about Gradiva, Barthes writes that the amorous experience assumes something of the same function as the analytic cure and that we must not underestimate the curative power of love in delusion. And later:

> The issue at stake in the Gradivian technique: [...] to recognize the subject in love as a subject, that is, to prove to him his own existence, his own value, and to want to teach him something about himself. This recognition must be indirect.

> (Barthes, 1977, p. 489)

Before Searles, Loewald and Ogden, speaking frankly of love in analysis (where in fact one never talks about anything else) was taboo because it was immediately likened to the "fire in the theatre", the image that Freud uses to embody the transgression of the rules of the setting. To say that analysis heals through a kind of indirect love is neither wrong nor exaggerated. Bion writes that the mother loves her baby with reverie. The best discussion of love in analysis I know is in an essay by Ogden entitled "Reading Harold Searles", included in the book *Rediscovering Psychoanalysis* (2008). Commenting on Searles's *Oedipal Love in the Countertransference*, Ogden argues that if the therapist is to successfully analyze oedipal love he must fall in love with the patient, recognizing that his desires can never be realized and that they will always remain in the sphere of feeling. After all, this is the same as observing in analysis the prohibition of incest, the only law common to all cultures and the law that forms the foundation of civilization. It is therefore, also the treatment of an artificiality that is in no way artificial.

Chetrit-Vatine (2012) talks about analysis as a situation of mutual seduction, but that obviously the analyst must be "ethical". Similarly, Julia Kristeva sees the transference as a "new love story", and the request for treatment as indicating a lack of love that can be filled only in the experience of the transference bond: "complaints, symptoms or fantasies are discourses of love directed to an impossible other always unsatisfactory, transitory, incapable of meeting my wants or desires" (Kristeva, 1985, p. 34). According to Jean Laplanche, the psychic birth of the infant is based on the mother's primary seduction.

THE ANALYTIC FIELD MODEL

This section deals with some of the main aspects of this way of understanding analysis, now broadly identified with the Pavia School, since other references can be found elsewhere in the book and those wishing to explore the subject in more depth can turn to the recommended reading section where we list some useful bibliographic references.

In short, and obviously at the cost of some simplification, one might say that we are dealing with an extreme version of the Freudian paradigm of dreams and the technique of floating attention★, which in the form mediated by Bion takes on its full meaning. It is true that much has changed since the time of classical psychoanalysis and the centrality of the oneiric component is now given an original interpretation. Among the new concepts we might mention: the unconscious as a psychoanalytic function of personality, in other words, how the mind gives a personal meaning, both emotionally and conceptually, to experience; the unconscious as something that is inaccessible and not repressed, that is to say, made up of internal operating schemes or implicit memories and not of psychic representations; dream work as an activity of symbolization and the essential equivalence of dreaming and thinking; the reconceptualization of the dichotomy between primary and secondary process, no longer seen as two qualitatively different ways of thinking, but as two polarities on a continuum; the adoption of a systematic principle of doubt; the model of how a mind develops starting from another mind and the quality of its capacity for reverie; the reformulation of the purpose of therapy, which is no longer to translate the unconscious into the conscious, but to "make" the unconscious, or to expand the mind's capacity to translate experience; emphasis on the development of psychic containers – functions and processes – rather than on the retrieval or discovery of psychic contents acting as foreign bodies vis-à-vis the psyche; the centrality given to psychic transformations, considered the most appropriate way to grasp what happens in the immediacy of the session, and the explanation of these transformations with the help of the theories of narratology; the centrality given to emotions rather than to the concept of drive in the theory of the development of the psyche.

It must be said that while reference to Bion remains central to the model of the analytic field, given how original and enlightening his clinical insights are, it would be difficult to imagine how to deploy his theories and his technical principles in everyday clinical practice if not by starting from the additions, clarifications and modifications, and from the original contributions made by the authors who took on the task of deepening and expanding his thought (the outstanding names in this context are Grotstein, Meltzer, Ogden and Ferro). Only thanks to them can we say that Bion's thought – which, in clinical terms, could be described as essentially Kleinian – is transformed into a series of innovative and, above all, easily transmissible tools (albeit not as easily as one might think), and not based only on the special talent that an analyst may or may not have. In our opinion, this is a distinctive feature of the analytic field model. The immediate, tactical purpose of these tools – think of the concepts of transformation in dreams, at play and in hallucinosis; the concepts of reverie, metaphor, dream flashes, bodily reveries; and then the concepts of dreams in the session, narrative derivatives of waking dream thought, characters in the session, etc. – is to expand the analyst's receptivity to the facts of the analysis and consequently his ability to help the patient make personal sense – private but shared – of experience. Generally speaking, the analyst tends to ask himself new questions rather than to give answers. In itself this is already a very powerful factor in the developmental transformation of the relationship, because it is obvious that new questions open up new perspectives of meaning and change the mutual affective investments at stake. The trademark of this kind of psychoanalysis is therefore its strong inclination to contribute to the theoretical developments of psychoanalysis, but at all events to privilege the moment when the clinical facts are confronted. This is the area in which even analysts who, as it were, speak different languages, can more easily dialogue in a profitable way and verify the added meaning that some theoretical tools rather than others enable us to procure.

Let us now return to the element that signals both the greatest continuity with Freud's psychoanalysis and the greatest discontinuity: the radical way of deploying the dream paradigm. On several occasions we have emphasized the key principle of analytic field theory on the basis of which virtually all events or facts of the analysis can be seen as related to multiple transference vectors that are activated in the immediacy of the session. The concept of "internal setting" refers precisely to the attitude of the analyst who considers every element of the text of the analysis and also of the setting as part of the analytic field and as a potential expression of the transference. By "internal setting" we mean not only uniformly suspended attention, but the possibility of regaining, after every (inevitable) interruption of the performance that is constantly staged in the theatre of analysis, a point of view that shows *in the field* that which apparently presents itself only as a fact, an event of present or past external reality or only as an element of the psychic reality of the analyst or patient. To adopt such a point of view simply means not to forget that analysis is concerned with the truth of the unconscious and of psychic reality.

The goal the analyst sets himself is not to decode content but to help the patient develop his alpha function, to think the previously unthinkable, that is, to retrieve aspects of himself which, because they cannot be processed, digested or alphabetized, are split off and projected outwards, so as to be able to transform them into alpha elements and oneiric thoughts – in essence, into representations, concepts and narratives that possess meaning. In this process the receptivity of the analyst's mind is essential, that is to say, his readiness to accept the projective identifications of the patient and to transform them using his capacity for reverie (which can also be sensory or bodily).

When this happens there follows a series of cycles in which the creative coupling of the minds of the two parties to the analytic dyad produce moments that are variously called encounters, emotional unison, "dyadic expansion of consciousness", psychic growth, and the like. The cycles could be described in technical jargon as oscillations between the paranoid-schizoid position and the depressive position (SP↔DP), container and contained (♀/♂) and negative capacity★/chosen fact★ (NC↔SF); in other words, these are the realization each time a transition from a situation of crisis, persecution, confusion or fragmentation to a position where scattered data is brought together, meaning is created and responsibility is assumed. This is how we manage to set in motion the work of symbolization and to make sure that the patient's mind, but ultimately also the analyst's, is able to bear heavier loads of pain, truth, anguish or "reality". The analyst tries as much as possible not to do the patient out of the invaluable opportunity to participate actively in this development. This is why he tends to use interpretations that are usually termed "weak" or "unsaturated". Rejecting the definitive closure of meaning, the unsaturated, open interpretation asks the other to engage in imaginative work. Dialogue can then evolve along unexpected lines. A welcoming atmosphere is created, where it is easier to pick up nuances; the gaze becomes sharper, the pleasure of playing the "psychoanalytic game" or the "game of the unconscious" is discovered. It is useful to deploy a rhetoric which is allusive (from the Latin *ad* + *ludere*, in other words, "to play"), evocative, and elliptical, one which suggests meaning without delivering it completely, leaving space to the other, to the unsaid, also to reticence, to eloquent silence, not opaque or closed in on itself; a silence that creates a concave, receptive space, whose opposite is not speech but noise, open to the unexpected and the unknown of the unconscious.

In order to orientate himself, the analyst can also use the compass of his theories. They can help him understand what is happening on the deep and unconscious emotional level; this means that he is constantly guided, not only by the patient's direct but also, especially, by his indirect signals. Thus, he also avoids changing the frame of reference of his discourse in a way that might be too premature and therefore traumatic. Basically this functions in the same way as the famous game invented by Winnicott for use in consultations with children: together analyst and child would draw scribbles on paper, each adding a line in turn, and seeing what figures would gradually take shape and what meaning they might express. This does not mean that there is never any loss of contact, errors, inevitable breakdowns in communication or "diseases" of the field. The setting itself is a vehicle that implies a certain necessary "violence", as well as containment, in the sense that it nevertheless requires compliance with certain rules.

The analyst listens to what the patient says, but also to his own explicit or only interior discourse, paying particular attention to the characters and the plots that develop, and which he sees as the unconscious narrative derivatives of the waking dream thought, the continual transformation of beta elements (proto-sensations and proto-emotions) into visual images (pictograms or alpha elements) that the mind is called upon to perform. At the same time, he considers that a "cloud of beta elements" not only embodies proto-sensory data waiting to be filtered by the alpha function of the mind, but also a sort of primitive container. Even the beta elements, like the emotional factors that produce a crystallization of meaning and each time lead on to a terrain of crisis, again open up new paths through the game of meaning. One also understands that a certain level of tolerable ambiguity becomes both an instrument and a goal in the sense of being synonymous with emotional maturity. Ultimately, beta elements convey drives, emotions and the transference. These are the factors that each time redraw the force lines in the field and determine its direction. Symbolization can only be seen in constant tension with its own un-doing, in the dialectic of interaction between two polarities of the couple – emotion and confusion, certainty and doubt.

Thus, dialogue, although the product of a generative grammar that is to be equated with the specific interpretive procedures of analytic work, tends, it is true, to take place on a superficial level. However, this is only apparent, since in actual fact it is shifted from the second or third level, less visible yet not to be neglected, as in the different layers of a palimpsest. The unconscious emotional truth, which on different occasions the interpretation aims to achieve, is mostly either implied or approached indirectly, because it is a reflection of the truth and not the absolute truth, the outcome of an ongoing negotiation.

The analytic field model leads to a style of work that places great trust in the power of speech, in the intrinsic faculty of the analytic device to lend weight, substance and density to the word; to restore it to a kind of auroral state that is close to the magic of poetic expression; to institute its own metaphors and languages. It should, however, be stressed that, while invaluable, analytic discourse is also perishable. Despite the analyst's best intentions, it can easily be debased into falsity and violence, and for this reason he is constantly called upon to vigilate over himself and his impulses and his feelings, and to interpret them using his ability to identify their unconscious meaning.

On the level of style, he will try to be natural, simple and spontaneous, while at the same time disciplined. Equally, the language he uses will aim at transparency and clarity. Deep down he is aware of the relative, provisional and conjectural character of his knowledge, which he knows can always be revised or amended. He seeks to be impervious to certainties, arrogance and assertiveness.

The patient experiences the analyst as a person who puts up with uncertainty, contradictions and complexity, who tolerates not understanding everything immediately and accepts having to look out onto the abyss opened up by the insignificance of the human condition. However, in the face of all this, he also has a method which he is confident will enable him to acquire – and help the other acquire – a new narrative competence and growth of thought.

Outlining such an attitude as an ideal model, which as we see it is minimalist and "kind" – a term on which we would like to confer a "theoretical-technical" quality, in the same way that Steiner holds that truth is either kind or not truth at all (2016) – even if it is firm, means spurning the oracular, mystical, ecclesiastical, scientistic or aestheticizing versions of psychoanalytic practice. What we would like to emphasize, however, is a theoretical and technical approach that is profoundly ethical. The analyst assumes maximum responsibility towards the patient, knowing that in the theatre of analysis, as Bion never tires of repeating, there is no way of avoiding pain, fear and danger. He thinks that the truth of the underlying solitude of the human condition must emerge and that ideally, at the conclusion of the analysis, as the patient takes his leave he will carry with him the secret of the illusory nature of the real, the sense of the transience of things or, as Searles (1965) would put it, the acceptance of the idea of the inevitability of pain and death. Basically, this is the same lucid pessimism that Freud expressed, or rather the sweetness of a well-tempered scepticism that in no way idealizes the negative.

PRIMITIVE STATES OF THE MIND AND THE INACCESSIBLE UNCONSCIOUS

Before going on to mention the so-called unrepressed unconscious, let us briefly recapitulate a few points. The Freudian model of the psyche is a unipersonal psychology, that is, it seeks to know the other by investigating his/her intrapsychic dynamics: conflicts, drives, the quality of internal objects, etc. Starting from the repetition in analysis of the long-established patterns relating to infantile neurosis, the so-called transference (this is what triggers remembering in the treatment), the analyst unveils to the patient his unconscious fantasies – for example, his incestuous desire for his mother – and in doing so counts on the intrinsically therapeutic value of knowledge.

In post-Freudian psychoanalysis, something important happens: in the 1970s, the relational paradigm begins to establish itself. The subject is born, as Hegel would have said, from a dialectic of recognition, from the desire for the other's desire. From birth the child is immersed in a cultural system that is provided by the mother; and indeed, as Winnicott said, there is no such thing as a child, there is only the mother-child couple.

Likewise, whatever happens in the session is now no longer seen as the product of a one-directional projection (transference) of aspects of the analysand's childish neurosis onto the white screen of a neutral analyst, but as something both old and totally new to which both actors-spectators on the analytic scene contribute, even though work starts from a basic asymmetry. Within a relational or intersubjective model, it becomes more difficult to translate the unconscious as a therapeutic tool. The analyst must now take into account his own ineliminable subjectivity and the contribution he makes to the creation of the facts he observes. He does not read/interpret the patient one-way, but rather, meaning becomes the result of negotiation.

However, as if this were not enough, things get more complex. The unconscious may also be structured as a language, as Lacan says. However, we must consider that it is not just a verbal language, because there is an older, prediscursive unconscious, which is not a repressed unconscious. It is an "unthought known" (Bollas, 1987), made up of memories that still bear the bodily impressions of the first relations with the object, of the life lived even before the ego was formed or developed (if we admit that it is already present at birth in a rudimentary form). By shifting their focus from drives to the relationship, analysts have increasingly come to realize that much of the pathology they have to deal with in clinical practice stems from dysfunctions connected to this level, to the level of a system of memories that does not translate into mental representations and is therefore not accessible to language, but rather as part of an aesthetics of being.

To get an idea of this, let us see how Ogden describes psychic birth or, one might say, the first psychic translation:

> the breast is not experienced as part of the mother's body that has a particular (visually perceived) shape, softness, texture, warmth, etc. Instead, (or more accurately, in dialectical tension with the experience of the breast as a visually perceived object), the breast as autistic shape is the experience of being a place (an area of sensation of a soothing sort) that is created, for example, as the infant's cheek rests against the mother's breast. The contiguity of skin surfaces creates an idiosyncratic shape *that is the infant at that moment*. In other words, the infant's being is, in this way, given sensory definition and a sense of locale.
>
> (Ogden, 1991, pp. 382–383)

We are dealing here with nothing less than the dawn of meaning, the first transference, the first metaphor – what happens when, as Nietzsche would have said, the similar equals the dissimilar. That which is other than oneself (difference) is experienced in terms of the self (identity). Bearing in mind, then, that the whole analytic situation, the so-called setting, can be symbolically equivalent to the mother's body, the child's first home and world, and that if the child's first "words" are tactile, they will always retain this sensory, or more properly, somatopsychic quality, even when they are an expression of symbolic thought.

This is why, as we have already pointed out several times elsewhere in this book, the model of therapeutic action has changed: if we are to help the patient integrate, it is no longer (only) a matter of translating contents (of meanings); for example, it is not a question of unveiling the latent thoughts within a dream or the unconscious reason behind a given act so as to fill the gaps in memory that render the symptom incomprehensible.

Now the analyst takes into account the model of the cheek/breast interface and is concerned about whether his interpretative interventions are tolerable or not, making sure that he avoids forcing meanings (differences) that are unsustainable for the ego. Promoting psychic growth is a matter of keeping pace, of being in unison: this is why interpretation in analysis now takes the form – to borrow an expression from Eco – of saying almost the same thing (which can be called weak, unsaturated or narrative interpretation); that is, it is like someone translating from one language to another who introduces acceptable elements of novelty at the same time as respecting the need for identity. And identity has to do not only with psychic contents but also with the frame around the painting, with the background against which the figure stands out, with the body and its emotions — and does not allow itself to be grasped from a purely logical-rational point of view.

In current psychoanalysis, analysts face more severe pathologies than in the past. They find themselves translating from an absent text, giving meaning to the "white noise" of the trauma, to the memories of the body that precede the ego. It is a matter of reconstructing the background from which the reflective consciousness emerges, of re-setting the margins, the frames within which the experience is organized; getting in tune with the music of events, with the inexpressible; restoring sense, which is also making sense for the first time: I live what you live/have experienced and I translate it into this form, which is perhaps better because it helps you get back in touch with split-off aspects of yourself. It is something that we can connect once more with the idea of rhythm, to the extent that rhythm is something that is felt and contributes to the creation of meaning, but does not allow itself to be uttered. This is why the aesthetic experience and the feeling of truth that we associate with it ultimately become a model for analytic work.

Remembering, therefore, is just as important as forgetting in the effort to survive pain. Thought itself is made of remembering and forgetting, that is to say, the capacity we have, and which naturally has its basis in the architecture of the brain, to grasp certain similarities while neglecting differences and thus the ability to construct categories, symbols and metaphors, in order to adapt and survive in the immediate context of experience.

The dividing line between health and illness does not so much run between remembering and forgetting, as between the ability and the inability to transform proto-emotions and proto-sensoriality into thought. There are memories that kill and memories that save. Those that kill or make ill are memories that hurt, that retain or take on a traumatic character, that is, that exceed the assumptive and transformative capacities of the individual. When there is an accumulation of undigested emotions, they become encapsulated in a symptom, taking the path from banal hypochondriacal concern to the "autoimmune" disintegration of the very apparatus of thought, from autistic isolation within extinguished memory that has the taste of an historical account to the most serious perversions.

The important thing is whether the emotions associated with memories can be contained by the psyche, that is, whether they can be subjected to the work of signification that is essentially based on the mechanisms of dream rhetoric as highlighted by Freud. But this ability is not given *a priori* at birth; it is the result of a long relationship in which the mother (or, to use the more accurate English term, the caregiver) makes available to the child her ability to think or engage in reverie; welcomes, transforms and sends back the projective identifications and toxic emotions which the child absorbs "by contagion", and thus allows this ability to develop as a real faculty. In this way we are able to "dream" or alphabetize experience, to draw up maps that make sense of experience. Facts become truly meaningful to us only when they are connected to emotions, which are obviously expressions of value systems, when they stop being sterile historical accounts and turn into narratives.

The persistence of this capacity is what helps the main character in Jelloun's novel (mentioned in Chapter 2, in the section entitled *Hysterics suffer from memories*) to survive the amputation of part of his identity, to start again from the darkness, which naturally, as Freud says, is an image of the absence of the other or not seeing the mother, and starting the psychic work necessary to regain the other. His struggle against the past does not end in the systematic and voluntary erasing of memories, because in order to survive he must also maintain and nurture a feeling of self. Here then, he begins to tell stories both to himself and to the prisoners in the neighbouring cells, pages and pages of the novels he had read in his youth and that he knew by heart (Hugo, Balzac, Camus) and also new stories invented there and then, or variations that he introduces on purpose. However, he does not perform this activity in absolute solitude. It is a bit like the work of weaving emotions and thoughts that is done in analysis in the face of something unthinkable or traumatic. This is his method of treatment. Like Scheherazade – and perhaps as we all do every day – he wards off death by giving a tolerable meaning to existence.

THE ANALYSIS OF CHILDREN AND ADOLESCENTS

Perhaps the reader will remember the strategy Quintus Fabius Maximus, known as the Delayer, adopted to win the war against Hannibal. A good parent faced with a child suffering from a medical emergency should also know how to temporize, in other words should ask the question: "What can I do? Why is this happening?" He or she should take some time and allow some time for the problem to go away, to solve itself. We believe this should be the first step. If, and only if, the suffering expressed as a symptom (and which could be expressed in many different ways) turns out to not be temporary, does it tend to become fixed and to restrict the child's life and ability to perform adequately. At this point the question becomes: "Who am I supposed to take my son to?" The best practice would be to turn to the professional figures with whom the child is most frequently in contact. The paediatrician who has been looking after the child will be able to tell whether it is a passing phenomenon, a symptomatic phenomenon, an existential malaise at that given moment or whether it is something that requires some kind of intervention.

This is exactly what a doctor would do when faced with any symptom, which may sometimes only require waiting, sometimes a minor and sometimes a more in-depth intervention. At this point this person will act as an intermediary and will recommend closer examination by a child neuropsychiatrist, a psychotherapist or a psychoanalyst.

All that is required is an opinion. No automatic response is triggered, along the lines of a certain symptom appears = psychotherapy, another symptom appears = doing analysis. Obviously, the consultation will result in a recommendation as to whether in that particular case with that particular child the path of therapy is the right one to follow or not. For example, if there were a problem of *pavor nocturnus* (a child who wakes up at night screaming in panic), this does not mean that the child should necessarily undergo analysis. Nightmares are a kind of indigestion of the mind. The thing to do would be to put the child on an emotional diet, to lighten its emotional load and in most cases the problem will solve itself. Many of the ailments or minor pathologies children suffer from appear and disappear with equal naturalness.

Then there are also cases in which a disorder manifests itself in the form of a fixed symptom and in ways that require specialized intervention.

Here, it might be useful to distinguish between age groups (generally speaking, between children and adolescents) and ask whether it is appropriate to turn to a therapy that seems to work on a plane of abstract, logical-rational communication, which is how adult analysis is sometimes understood, or whether there might not be something simpler. In our view this is an important question, precisely because analysis should be a simple thing. The analysis of adults should be exactly like the analysis of children: absolutely simple, something that has to do with emotions and feelings. With adults the aim of achieving simplicity is a challenge both in terms of the psychoanalyst's career and for the patient.

With a child, all this is normally easier. Generally speaking, the great adventure of child analysis began with Melanie Klein and with the discovery that play is, in practice, the equivalent of dreaming. Certainly, therapeutic work with a child does not follow the path of reasoning but essentially takes place through play, play which also involves the analyst himself. Without being aware of it, through play the patient sets up representations of psychic functioning and dysfunctioning, problems, sufferings and elements of his internal world. By participating in this playing activity, the analyst is able to find, together with the child, solutions, outlets and transformations in relation to the things that he, as it were, puts on stage. This happens without the young patient having any idea about what he is showing in make-believe form or being aware of the real answers that the analyst will provide through play.

There is another tool which can be used in child analysis, and that is drawing. The child can draw without being aware that the drawing (which should be as spontaneous as possible) is something that enacts the state of his inner world, the state of his relationship with the analyst and what is going on or what is being blocked or unblocked in his inner world.

So, we have these two perfectly simple methods: play and drawing, neither of which should be pushed in any particular direction. As long as this is the case, the prerequisites for spontaneous play and drawing are created, and these will become the primary tool to be used in child analysis. The child has absolutely no idea of the process that is unfolding or the transformations that are taking place. His perception will be that he is drawing or playing with someone who is playing with him. Classic instruments such as dreams may also come into play, but usually children prefer drawing or telling stories or playing rather than recounting their dreams. The child will be able to report things that happen in his daily life, at school, even in dreams, should they occur. The analyst should avoid making complicated or cerebral comments, but rather interact with the child in the simplest way possible so as to turn the child's words into tools that convey knowledge of his suffering and above all that solve his problem. Logically enough, different approaches can be followed and not necessarily the psychoanalytic path. The potential advantage of psychoanalysis, however, lies in the fact that it is practised by someone who has undergone very specific training that enables him to look beyond the symptom and to see what the problems and their roots may be.

To take an example: enuresis (when a child wets the bed despite having learnt how to control his sphincter muscles). The interesting point is that the analysis will clearly show how the symptom is always the expression of something else.

Let us take a 12-year-old boy: what is he talking about through this symptom? He is probably speaking of an incontinence of certain emotional aspects that he cannot hold back, that "break free" and are evacuated. So, the problem is no longer the child's enuresis but how to enable this person to better contain his emotional states. And this will be an integral element in resolving the problem in hand. Children will not need analysis if they suffer from small temporary symptoms such as headaches, school phobias or similar disorders.

However, they will need therapy if they show signs of suffering that might veer towards something more organized. It will be necessary to intervene using an appropriate therapy if a child presents symptoms of anorexia, which might then take the form of a serious disorder, or if a child, despite not showing any pathological traits, begins to engage in obsessive behaviours that prevent him from living a normal life, from playing with other children and learning. The moment non-transitory manic rituals enter the scene (transitory rituals are absolutely normal in all children; these include not stepping on the gaps between tiles, or performing small rituals before falling asleep, before an exam or any other anxiety-inducing event), which prevent the child from studying, making friends or having fun, it would be hard not to intervene. Or in the case of a phobia, not just a fear of spiders or dogs, but a serious phobia of dirt that might curtail a person's life, then we should intervene. Not to mention a child who experiences disperceptive phenomena (hearing voices that are not there or seeing things that do not exist).

Similar considerations apply in the case of adolescents. They too may experience physiological turbulences that do not make it necessary to trouble an analyst; it is enough to help parents to be on their guard and to monitor the problem, to reflect on it and to help solve it. There are, however, other situations where there is a risk that symptoms may become fixed and make the adolescent's everyday life painful. In this case it would be a pity to make an adolescent suffer when the remedy exists. Sometimes, just a few sessions are enough; this is what is called a prolonged or short consultation.

There are several situations in which we witness the forming of panic attacks, anorexia, severe obsessive or depressive symptoms, the appearance of signs of possible psychotic breakdowns – all of which make it necessary for the analyst to intervene rapidly to prevent the whole situation from getting out of control.

Just now we were speaking of depression, which often forms part of an adolescents experience for some periods. But what are the symptoms or signs of depression in young children?

It must be said, incidentally, that depression is the most frequent companion that human beings have; we would also add that mental health often borders on a mild depressive state.

A mild state of depression is the norm for many of us. There are people who cannot stand this state and so try all the antidepressants that (fortunately) life can offer. But what is depression and how does it occur – in adults, in adolescents, in children?

In children it manifests itself clearly when the child does not want to get up in the morning, is always tired and finds going to school a great effort. A young patient was unable to write the number eight straight up (8) and could only do it "lying down" (∞) – as the sign of infinity. Only by grasping the depressive value of this sign did it become possible to resolve the problem. Sometimes play might slow down, the child might suffer from a certain inertia or tiredness, then there are all the other somatic equivalents of depression, in other words, the symptoms that are manifestations of masked depression although they are not easily recognizable as such. Some of the most common examples of depressive equivalents include headaches and certain inexplicable febrile upturns.

So, is there a big difference between psychoanalysis for children and for adults?

The answer is a definite "no"! Different languages are used: verbal communications for the adult patient, play and drawing for the child. Child analysis will focus on the process of developing tools for thinking, feeling and dreaming, just as in adult analysis. This is particularly evident in the case of those analytic models that seek to develop communicative potential rather than the supposed development of the mind through different phases.

Furthermore, the analysis of children has made it easier to access preverbal phenomena and the more primitive levels of minds in relation to each other for all age groups. Recent works, such as those by Salomonsson (2014), provide evidence of breakthroughs in therapy with children of only a few months (helped by the presence of the mother), which were previously unthinkable.

ONE PSYCHOANALYSIS OR MANY?

Those seeking to explore the world of psychoanalysis can easily fall prey to a certain scepticism upon discovering how many different schools and theoretical orientations are subsumed under this umbrella term. For analysts too, this Babel of psychoanalytic models is a cross to bear. From time to time the question of a common ground in psychoanalysis re-emerges in the literature. For some the plurality of perspectives is a mark of scientific poverty, for others a sign of richness.

Certain critics of psychoanalysis – but sometimes even its supporters – tend to not bother to keep up to date or even to acquire a minimum level of knowledge about the history of its concepts and models. They start from ideas and principles that have long been abandoned and completely ignore the most recent developments. In other words, they take up a position in a kind of atemporal dimension, which they obviously find more comfortable. It would be more correct, however, to start from what, even given the variety of different points of view, is regarded as the state of the art. It is difficult to know why something that would be inadmissible in any other scientific field, even in the human sciences, appears normal in psychoanalysis.

THE BABEL OF THE UNCONSCIOUS

It is nevertheless true that, sometimes, the impression is that everything is kept and nothing is really left behind once and for all. This is true and not true at the same time and depends on the nature of the discipline. Why is this the case? Because the object of study of psychoanalysis is the most complex that exists: the human mind. There are aspects of our being human that cannot be translated into words and which must instead be addressed and thematized in an indirect, "musical", artistic way. From this point of view, every great author of psychoanalysis is also quite simply a writer. He creates a world. He offers a version of the object of study filtered through his subjectivity. At least with regard to this more aesthetic or intuitive part, Freud's psychoanalysis can never be completely "outdated" – nor can that of Klein, Winnicott, or Bion. All these perspectives could be seen in a positive light – as is ambiguity in poetry or differences in style in painting. Freud's fascinating journeys into the world of dreams (even if we no longer work as he did, for example, systematically asking patients to produce associations for all the details of the dream scene); the horror "films" "shot" by Klein with newborn infants as leading characters, but which are themselves monstrous in their obsessive search for meaning; Winnicott's surprising mixture of simplicity and unsettling originality; the illuminating paradoxical nature of certain formulas invented by Bion the "Indian" – if we ever did without them, we would surely be reduced to a kind of depersonalized psychoanalytic Esperanto. It would be neither desirable nor feasible. Inclining ever more towards the logical, rational, "scientific" pole of psychoanalysis would amount to throwing the baby out with the bathwater. Perhaps the factors that least lend themselves to being expressed in words, the so-called non-specific factors, are the most important in treatment. Psychoanalysis is and, unless it is distorted into a kind of absurd neuropsychoanalysis, will therefore remain a kind of in-between art. After all, like medicine, it too feeds on data, just like the exact sciences, but then the cure in itself is an art. If all goes well, there are guidelines upon which most members of the community of researchers interested in a certain area can agree.

That said, there remains the task of explaining more coherently than usual why all models of psychoanalysis have the concept of truth at their centre. In our opinion this happens for various reasons that perhaps relational, Bionian and Winnicottian psychoanalysis allows us to develop within a broader epistemological framework.

The most important authors have put their own idiosyncratic spin on psychoanalytic theory. In the early years of the psychoanalytic movement this was due in part to Freud's intolerance of dissent and views other than his own. Over time some of the brightest students departed and founded their own schools; these included Jung, Adler, and Reich. Some stayed in the IPA but were marginalized, like Ferenczi. Others, such as Meltzer and Bion, moved away from purely psychoanalytic institutions towards the end of their lives.

But let us now draw a rough map of the different psychoanalytic approaches that play a part on the contemporary scene. First of all, it must be said that the parent society, the International Psychoanalytical Association, established by Freud in 1910, on the occasion of the International Congress at Nuremberg and which elected the Italian analyst Stefano Bolognini as its president for the four-year period 2013–17, still has around 12000 members and is present mainly in the Americas and in Europe. The Asian countries (Korea, China, Japan, India) and the Middle East (Iran) have started to come to the fore in the last few years. Since the fall of the Berlin Wall, psychoanalysis has flourished rapidly throughout Eastern Europe and Russia.

TOWARDS A NEW "COMMON GROUND"?

In a recent article, Otto Kernberg (2011), an authoritative analyst and former president of the IPA, named in this regard ego psychology, the galaxy of relational psychoanalysis, and the Italian post-Bionians(!). While this may be a valid list for a first stab at orientation, on closer examination things are much more fragmented and second- or third-degree level differences emerge. At all events, probably due to the Internet, the vertiginous increase in transnational exchanges, conferences and the internationalization of magazines (above all, the "International Journal of Psychoanalysis"), the impression is that the pre-conditions are in place for gradually developing a new common ground. In some ways even ego psychology has come very close to relational models. As usual, elements of continuity and discontinuity can be seen both on a diachronic and a synchronic axis. For example, Freud "discovered" psychic reality and transference; Klein mapped its geography and, like an anthropologist, identified its indigenous populations, and with the concept of unconscious phantasy ushered in its systematic exploration; Bion broadened this concept of the mind to make it bi-personal or groupal and brought the analyst's subjectivity into play. With Bion and Winnicott, the theory of the mind became a strong social theory. The following section looks at the Italian tradition of psychoanalysis.

PSYCHOANALYSIS IN ITALY

"Das Italienreisen ist nämlich nicht so ganz ohne Beschwerden, wie man sich's erwartet"

("This traveling in Italy is not so completely without difficulties, as one might expect")

This quotation is taken from a letter Freud wrote to his wife Martha dated September 7, 1886, from Torre del Gallo (or Tower of Galilei, which belonged to a nearby villa where Galileo spent his last years of life), close to Florence, and only recently discovered by Harold Blum (1999), director of the Sigmund Freud Archives of the Library of Congress in Washington. In it, Freud mentions Italy's bad railways, its wonderful cuisine, the beauty of the sights, and the wide-spread presence of works of art that are found almost everywhere. "The memorials stand around in half-dozens on the street," he writes, to the point of stunning the observer, making him experience "the whole dizziness of southern beauty" ("der ganze … Schwindel südlicher Schönheit") (ibid., pp. 1253–1254), an expression that somehow foreshadows the Stendhal syndrome which, according to contemporaries, would strike tourists particularly susceptible to aes-thetic emotion. Equally anticipatory is Freud's fascination with the tower-observatory of Galileo, a scientific figure one can easily see him identifying with. This house, which had been partly transformed into a museum, is where he decided to stay with his brother Alexan-der after having rented three rooms from the owner of the building: "The whole magnificence will only last another three days. On Fri-day morning we will telegraph our trip home, a trip during which we will probably atone for all our sins" (ibid., p. 1255).

The ironic tone with which he associates Italy with sin and guilty pleasure is telling and gives some clues to Freud's state of mind when he looked upon it as the locus of the unconscious. Antonietta and Gérard Haddad (1995) have suggested that Italy played a special role in the discovery of the unconscious and the Oedipus complex, which took place precisely in the period of Freud's self-analysis and his first trips to Italy. The land of beauty and sensuality would have represented for Freud the forbidden place of the mother's body. The expression "Amar Italia", which contains a kind of anagram of the names of Freud's wife, Martha, and his mother Amalia, and the inhibition that for a long time held Freud away from Rome (which in Italian is *amor*/love backwards, and whose topography he would spend whole days studying, as if hypnotized) would support their thesis.

But, in spite of the great "love" (Lacan) or "passion" (Gay) that, between "Grand Tour" and incestuous fantasies, Freud felt for Italy, as evidenced by his many trips there (twenty!), the penetration of psychoanalysis in the "Bel Paese" was never easy, indeed it was decidedly "uncomfortable" ("nicht … ohne Beschwerden"), due to a series of concomitant specific factors. Firstly, Catholic culture, which – as it did for Galileo's revolutionary theses – had long placed psychoanalysis on the index on account of Freud's materialism, the Darwinian imprint of his thought and his so-called pansexualism; then the philosophical idealism expressed by Benedetto Croce, the greatest Italian philosopher of the last century, and his pupil Giovanni Gentile, who disparaged the psychology and the positivist spirit that animates scientific research in favour of aesthetic and historical knowledge; finally, the organicist orientation of psychiatry at the time, dominated by Cesare Lombroso, the founder of criminal anthropology, who sought the stigmata of "psychic degenerations" in somatic traits.

Subsequently, the spread of psychoanalysis was hindered by the general isolation imposed on Italian society by its Fascist period, which, after an initial ambiguity, became ever more intolerant, and then, after the Second World War, its rejection by some Marxist-inspired political and cultural forces who considered it bourgeois, irrational, and abstract. It is immediately clear, then, why the gateway to psychoanalysis in Italy was Trieste: a frontier city, Central European, Slavic, and Italian, German but with a significant Jewish presence, an integral part of the Austro-Hungarian Empire, to which it served as a port until 1918. One can see as prophetic the presence in that same city of a very young Freud, a student in his third year of medicine in Vienna, on a scholarship for a few months in 1876 at the experimental zoological station that had recently been established to conduct research on the gonads of eels – the subject which became the basis for his first scientific publication.

Another figure from Trieste was Edoardo Weiss, the "spreader" in Italy of the psychoanalytic "plague". Coming from a Jewish family, as did almost all of the first Italian analysts, Weiss, born in 1889, studied medicine and psychiatry in Vienna, where he came into contact with Freud and was analyzed by Paul Federn, later to becoming a member of the IPA (1913) and of the Viennese Psychoanalytic Society. To give an idea of the climate that reigned in Trieste, it was here that James Joyce lived for sixteen years, until July 1920 when, aged thirty-eight, he left the city where he wrote and published all his early works and where he wrote the first episodes of *Ulysses*. We know that Joyce met Weiss's brother, Ottocaro, and Italo Svevo (Ettore Schmitz), and from mid-1907 he in fact became Svevo's private English teacher and later his close friend. Svevo is the author of *La coscienza di Zeno (Zeno's conscience)*, one of the masterpieces of world literature inspired by psychoanalysis, which would later serve as a model for the novels *Incubus* by Giuseppe Berto and *Portnoy's Complaint* by Philip Roth. Finally, Trieste was where Umberto Saba, one of the greatest Italian poets of the first half of the twentieth century, lived, who was also influenced by his encounter with psychoanalysis and the analysis he did with Weiss in his practice in Via San Lazzaro 8.

In 1931 was the publication of Weiss's *Elementi Di Psicoanalisi (Elements of Psychoanalysis)* (Weiss, 1931) with a Preface by Freud. And it was Weiss himself who founded the Italian Society of Psychoanalysis (SPI) in Rome on October 1, 1932. One of its honorary members was Levi Bianchini, who, in Teramo (Abruzzo), had already proposed the society's first constitution in 1925, and who had been capable of having it welcomed three years later into the bosom of the IPA. The new society only lasted a short time. Already, in 1934, the *Rivista italiana di psicoanalisi*, after only two years, had to cease publication, as Jones (1953, p. 29) recounts, apparently after direct intervention by the Catholic Church. In 1938 the introduction of Italy's racial laws meant psychoanalysis was condemned as a "Jewish science", and the society was disbanded. From 1939 to 1945, the year of liberation from the Nazi occupation, psychoanalysis in Italy ceased to exist. In 1939, like many other European analysts, Weiss was forced to move to the United States, to be precise to Chicago, where he lived until 1970, working for a long time with Franz Alexander.

The society reorganized itself and was officially reconstituted in 1947. The year before the first Congress had been held in Rome on the subject of aggression(!). The *Rivista di psicoanalisi*, the official organ of the Society began to be published again in 1955. To give a numerical parameter, in 1964 the SPI included twenty-seven members and an almost equal number of associates. Today, the total number is about 1000, counting the various categories of members and candidates. The leading figures in Italian psychoanalysis in the post-war period were Weiss's students: Nicola Perrotti (from Abruzzo), Emilio Servadio (from Rome) as well as, Cesare Musatti (from Veneto) and Alexandra Wolff Stomersee, Princess Tomasi di Lampedusa. I have specified the geographical origin of some of the first Italian Freudians because provincialism can be seen as a compelling key to understanding the paths of development – the "journeys", as it were – of psychoanalysis in Italy.

One of these paths started off from as far away as Russia: Alessandra Tomasi di Lampedusa, daughter of a high dignitary at the court of Tsar Nicholas II, spent the first twenty years of her life in St. Petersburg, trained in Berlin at the Psychoanalytic Institute headed by Karl Abraham and in 1934 moved to Palermo, the city of her second husband, the author of *Il Gattopardo (The Leopard)*, the novel on which Luchino Visconti's famous film was based. The presence of this fascinating cosmopolitan figure in a city located at the opposite end of the peninsula from Trieste makes Palermo into another example of a "psychoanalytic province", an environment that fostered the development of some outstanding analysts, including Francesco Corrao, the person responsible for spreading the name of Bion and for paving the way for the study of groups.

In the second half of the last century, psychoanalysis in Italy grew not only in terms of numbers, as already mentioned, but also as a cultural phenomenon. Freudian theories began increasingly to permeate society, to the point almost of becoming "fashionable". Although they succeeded in overcoming much resistance, success was never complete (nor was it perhaps desirable if we take this fact as an indication of the "sulphurous" persistence, radicality, and effectiveness of psychoanalysis). For some time, the influence of ego psychology, in parallel with the dominance of this same model in the United States, was overwhelming. Over time, other influences were added. A number of analysts trained in London and went on to introduce the ideas of Melanie Klein and Anna Freud. Groups were formed that took inspiration from the ideas of Lacan. Bion and then Meltzer held seminars in Italy that left their mark. Matte Blanco came from Chile to settle in Rome in 1966 and became an influential figure. However, in the 1960s and 1970s the aristocratic complexion of the Italian Psychoanalytic Society (SPI) gradually led to it becoming isolated, not only from the academic world and psychiatric institutions but also from other national societies and even from the IPA itself.

The landscape has changed enormously in recent years, especially as a result of the introduction of the new law on the training of psychotherapists. The SPI has seen its membership grow considerably. There are now eleven centres across Italy and not only in large cities, a demonstration of its enviable vitality in the spheres of science, education, and cultural life in general. But above all it is now better able to exchange of ideas with institutions with whom it shares a scientific and cultural heritage.

GLOSSARY

Alpha elements These are the product of the transformation of *beta* elements (proto-sensoriality) performed by the *alpha* function of the mind. *Alpha* elements (representations) can be stored in memory, can connect with each other and can also generate dream thoughts.

Alpha function This is the psychic function that transforms *beta* elements into *alpha* elements, and as such we know very little about how it operates. In essence it is the ability of the mind to give meaning to experience once it has entered the register of the symbolic. The child can only acquire this ability from the mother or her substitute (caretaker).

Beta elements These are proto-sensations or proto-emotions awaiting transformation into *alpha* elements (mainly images) through the *alpha* function of the subject. When this "digestion" of the effects produced on the individual by a set of external and internal stimuli fails, *beta* elements can accumulate and give rise to various symptoms and pathologies. Bion imagines the transformation from *beta* to *alpha* as analogous to the process of digestion. Also important is Bion's decision to designate these elements using letters of the (Greek) alphabet, a reminder that everything has to do with the typically human way of making sense of experience – in other words, through language.

Compromise formation   The psychic contents that the individual finds himself forced to repress because they are subject to the action of the super-ego coming from the unconscious tend to resurface in consciousness as symptoms. However, this occurs only in a distorted form that renders them no longer recognizable because psychic defences have interfered with them. At this point they typically represent compromise formations, that is to say, elements that are at one and the same time the result, both of the expression and the fulfilment of a forbidden unconscious desire and of the needs of the defences. Dream elements and the ensemble of products of the unconscious are of the same nature.

Container/contained   Thought up by Bion, this formula, used to describe the nature and quality of the link between two terms, is brilliant both in its simplicity and its correspondence to the experience of practical life. Examples of concrete relationships (♀♂ – Bion also uses the symbols for female and male) are: mouth/nipple, vagina/penis, group/individual, mother/child etc. Container/contained relations are always multiple and reciprocal, as well as being virtually infinite if we also consider the small scale of interaction. The child contains in its mouth the nipple, which contains milk, while at the same time it is held by the arms of the mother, both existing in broader contexts that sustain and support them, and so on. ♀♂ is an extremely powerful and versatile tool; one might even say it is almost obvious. If it is heir to the concept of projective identification, then it is reborn as a sexual metaphor, which can also be seen from the symbols chosen by Bion to represent it, or as a metaphor of the mind as a digestive apparatus. It immediately gives an idea of what can happen if too much content ("contained") is forced into an inadequate container – or also, vice versa, if the container has become infinite and is no longer really able to accommodate and give form (meaning) to the contained.

Depressive position   Like the paranoid-schizoid (SP) position, this is a concept that comes from Kleinian psychoanalysis. It is used to indicate two essential aspects. One, functional/dynamic, refers to a state of psychic organization in which feelings of "depression" prevail due to the lessening of primitive omnipotence implicit in a process of psychic integration. The second is developmental/structural in kind and refers to a stage in the development of the psyche (around the middle of the first year of life) by which time the child has realized that a good object and a bad object can be united in the same person, and this makes him feel remorse for attacks on the latter. The fear of being attacked leads to the fear of losing the object, which has now become a "total" object. The process described by the concept of the depressive position therefore relates to the achievement of affective ambivalence.

Dream work   The German term *Traumarbeit* is often used to refer to the rhetorical mechanisms at work in dream construction as identified by Freud: condensation (*Verdichtung*), displacement (*Verschiebung*), considerations of representability (*Rücksicht auf Darstellbarkeit*) and secondary revision (*sekundäre Bearbeitung*). Dream activity masks the latent thoughts of the dream that may disturb sleep and transforms them into manifest images that have lost their disquieting content. However, it is possible to work back to this content by undoing the dream work using the dreamer's associations. Condensation refers to the fact that a single image can represent an amalgam of several images, as in metaphor; displacement refers to the transfer of investment (presumed energy that can slip from one representation to another) from one image to another (the equivalent of metonymy). Figurability, or "considerations of representability", refers to the transformation into primarily visual images, while "secondary revision" indicates a kind of final editing process that lends a certain coherence and comprehensibility to the whole (thereby approaching the quality of a daydream).

Drive   This is perhaps the most fundamental concept in Freudian psychoanalytic theory (energy-and-drive theory). The drive (*Trieb*) is a psychic impulse that has its source in the body and is in search of a given object so as to lower the tension that has been generated. Basically it is a somatic process that gives rise to psychic excitement in the form of representations and affects and which leads to the putting into effect of behaviours designed to placate (or satisfy) it. The drive can, as it were, meet several different fates: it can be repressed, transformed into its opposite or sublimated. It must be distinguished from the concept of instinct, which refers to an innate, fixed and automatic response to a given stimulus. Drives, on the other hand, even if they are rooted in the body, are also an expression of the cultural nature of human beings, as they send their "representatives" to the psyche and contribute in this way to its creation. There is the idea that it presses on the psyche so as to transform somatic excitement and that, at the same time, the work carried out on the psyche is what helps to distinguish it. The main groups of drives are aggressive or sexual in nature.

Evenly suspended attention Freud coined the concept of evenly suspended attention to refer to what he considered the ideal listening attitude of the analyst. The English term has entered Italian terminology as a calque ("attenzione uniformemente sospeso"), alongside the accepted "attenzione fluttuante" (literally, "floating attention"). What is meant by the term? The analyst listens without privileging *a priori* any particular element of the patient's discourse and leaving himself open to being in some way surprised by original meaning effects, by the play of signifiers, by unexpected events of every kind and nature. It is a way of making the unconscious work, which shows that for Freud the unconscious was never simply a repository where unspeakable and sleazy things were stowed away. It is clear that this is above all a way of making room for what at first appears inessential or insignificant. It is equally clear that this is a goal towards which to strive asymptotically but which will probably never be fully attained. Freud's idea takes on a particular meaning in Lacanian psychoanalysis due to the close equivalence the latter established between the mechanisms of the unconscious and the mechanisms of language.

Libido Shortened form of *libido sexualis*, containing the Latin word for "desire". Freud uses this term to refer to the psychic expression of the sex drive ("the dynamic manifestation [of the sexual instinct] in mental life"). It gives a measure of the strength of the sex drive as a force that causes the organism to strive towards a goal or to seek an object that will release the tension generated by somatic excitation.

Metapsychology The complex of theories with which the various models of psychoanalysis represent psychic functioning that is not accessible to observation because it is situated beyond conscious experience. Falling within metapsychology are theories about the structuring of the mind into areas, agencies, drives, energy flows, defence mechanisms, and so on.

Negative capability Expression used by Bion to refer to the ability of the analyst to listen to the patient without looking too soon for preconceived meanings. Paradoxically, the analyst should rather disavow remembering or desiring anything or even understanding.

The formula is designed to indicate the state of mind most conducive to intuiting the unconscious emotional experience that patient and analyst go through in analysis. It is no more than a new way of saying that the analyst should listen to the patient in a state of floating or evenly suspended attention. Obviously, the expression takes on other nuances within a new theoretical framework that is no longer Freudian.

Neurosis   Type of psychic disorder in which the subject does not present the severe symptoms of psychosis and therefore does not lose contact with reality. Examples include obsessive, phobic and hysterical neuroses, anxiety neuroses, etc. A neurosis originates from a psychic conflict between desire and defence. Symptoms express this conflict in symbolic form.

Object   In psychoanalysis the term "object" is used mainly to indicate the person with whom the subject, the individual, enters a relationship, as a sexual object, object of love, etc. In general, therefore, it does not have the meaning of "thing" as in everyday language. The drive seeks in the object its goal or its own satisfaction. Because of its purely speculative nature and relative distance from clinical experience, metapsychology (it would in fact be more appropriate to talk of metapsychologies, given that every original author, to some extent, constructs his own), or part of it, is the subject of heated disputes between analysts.

Paranoid–schizoid position   Like the concept of depressive position (DP), this term belongs to Kleinian psychoanalysis. It is used to refer to two essential aspects. One, functional/dynamic, refers to a state of psychic organization in which feelings of persecution and disorientation prevail over the possibility of making sense of current experience. The second is developmental/structural in type and refers to a stage of psychic development (the first four months of life) in which the infant perceives the object as split into a good object and a bad object. Feelings of anxiety and persecution prevail due to fear of being attacked and destroyed by the latter.

Procedural memory   This expression is used to refer to memories that are not deposited as linguistic meanings (semantic or verbal) or as representations (images) but in the form of motor or emotional patterns. These are therefore silent traces, forms of "tacit" memory – unconscious, implicit, non-biographical and non-declarative. Being the result of past experiences, they are mostly expressed in actions, for example, cycling, playing tennis or playing a musical instrument.

Projection   By "projection", a term that has also entered every-day language, we mean the unconscious fantasy harboured by the individual that he can get rid of psychic contents that are unpleasant to the super-ego (such as feelings and desires) and which he is unwilling to recognize as its own, and to attribute them to the other. It is therefore a defence mechanism that comes into play to relieve the psyche of excessive emotional burdens. The price the subject then pays is that these contents return as realities.

Projective identification   Coined by Melanie Klein, the concept of projective identification, as opposed to the simple concept of projection, emphasizes the idea of the development of a fantasy whereby the subject insinuates himself partially or totally into the other (for this reason, "identification") to control him from the inside. The distinction may seem subtle or even non-existent but becomes meaningful if related to the different psychoanalytic models developed by Freud and Klein, respectively, each with their own emphasis on the intrapsychic and early relational perspective. Later this concept becomes clearer as it takes on an increasingly intersubjective colouring. Bion sees it as a psychic mechanism that is not only pathological but also physiological, as a normal mode of communication between individuals. Ogden further accentuates this aspect by pointing out that it is not just a limited phenomenon in the context of a pure fantasy of the subject, but that it also engages an effective interpersonal pressure to force the other to receive the projected contents.

Psychosis   Psychosis refers to a psychic illness in which the subject loses all or part of his contact with reality. Typically, delusions and hallucinations, in other words, false thoughts and wrong perceptions, can present themselves temporarily or chronically. Examples of psychosis are paranoia and schizophrenia.

Repression   An act that consists of maintaining or rendering unconscious certain psychic contents (thoughts, images, memories) linked to a drive and in conflict with other needs of the subject, mostly of a moral nature. It is therefore a way of removing elements that could cause displeasure or pain. However, these elements do not remain inert but continue to exert an influence on psychic life. Typically they press to return to consciousness and thus give rise to symptomatic formations. Common and banal examples are so-called Freudian slips or parapraxes (mistaken actions caused by the influence of complexes of repressed representations).

Selected fact   This is the element that demands attention and can sometimes suddenly make sense of what is happening in the relationship between patient and analyst on the unconscious emotional plane. In other words, it is the unexpected stimulus that, to put it in Kleinian terminology, prompts a shift from the paranoid-schizoid (SP) position to the depressive position (DP), from the feeling of persecution that comes from the painful experience of not being able to make sense of the experience, to the feeling instead of having found an illuminating and coherent meaning. In order to arrive at new meanings, however, each time it is necessary to go through further moments in which one has the impression of not understanding. The cycle is destined to repeat itself indefinitely.

Subject   This term has a long history in philosophy and generally refers to the individual as an aware being (capable of thinking thoughts). Freud levels a corrosive attack on the classic (Cartesian) concept of the subject by highlighting its limits: because of the importance that the unconscious life assumes, the ego, announces Freud, is not master in his own house.

Sublimation   Another term that has become current in everyday language, sublimation indicates the human capacity to forgo satisfying drives in favour of socially approved activities. Essentially, this means being able to convert the sex drive – in Freud's writings the recurrent "synonym" of sublimation is "sexual abstinence" – into something non-sexual and to change its object and goal. The new goal is "psychically related" to the original one but "higher and therefore unassailable" (Freud, 1909, p. 146); it is "socially valuable" (ibid., p. 171) because it concerns specifically human and socially approved functions and activities. It is not that direct sexual satisfaction has no social value for the individual, but that which is achieved by sublimation is of value for more than one person (without wishing to imply that for others it may have no value or or may even be condemned). Sublimation is thus a "transformed passion", in which the force of the drive has been mitigated, "tamed" (Freud, 1929, p. 571); it takes a different direction and aims at "a finer and higher joy" (ibid.), albeit of a much lower intensity than the direct satisfaction of cruder impulses, and such as not to "shake our bodily existence" (ibid.). Freud uses the theory of sublimation to explain the nature of artistic activity and aesthetic experience.

Transference   A patient hates or loves the analyst as if he were the father or mother of his childhood. He invests him with the same passion that he had when he was a child. This is transference (or in Italian *traslazione*, in German *Übertragung*). It is an unconscious and arbitrary transfer of feelings from one situation to another: more precisely, it affects impulses, affections and unpleasant thoughts because they are linked to a forbidden and distantly repressed desire (Le Guen, 2008). Initially, Freud saw it as a pathological process, a painful act of self-understanding, resistance that had to be fought against and eliminated. He called transference a *mésalliance*, using the French term used to indicate marriage with a person of a lower social status. Later, he was to change his mind. In 1912, in *Recommendations to Physicians Practising Psycho-analysis* (Freud, 1912), he referred to it as the "middle kingdom" (*Zwischenreich*) of analysis, something that lies between illness and reality. Transference is "artificial"; depending on the point of view, it is a surrogate, an expedient, an illusion. As an intermediate region it is a temporary and virtual "gym", but for this reason, he explained, it is "accessible to intervention" and can be the locus of infinite transformations (Freud, 1914a). With time, Freud went further and also acknowledged the truth and authenticity of transference. If a somewhat compulsive, pathological love appears, it is only because it is more delusional than normal love, which is also often ambivalent and likewise follows its infantile prototype. At all events, dealing with transference is like handling explosive material in a chemistry lab!

Waking dream thought   From a certain point of view this is the egg of Columbus. Human beings have always known that they dream even when awake. They have even asked the question – for example, through Descartes or the great literature of the Baroque age – whether waking might not in fact be a dream mode. Freud put dreams at the centre of his model of psychic life, since the method of free association is nothing other than a way of inducing a kind of hypnosis, of making people dream in order to gain access to the unconscious. However, it is only with Bion that the notion of the essential continuity between nocturnal and diurnal dreams becomes a theoretical cornerstone around which to build a new psychoanalytic paradigm and a new technique of treatment.

SUGGESTED READINGS

Regarding the birth of psychoanalysis we recommend: Henri F. Ellenberger (1970), *The Discovery of the Unconscious: The History and Evolution of Dynamic Psychiatry*, Basic Books, New York.

Among the many biographies of Freud: *Peter Gay* (1988), *Freud: A Life for Our Time*, WW Norton, New York; Ernest Jones (1974), *The Life and Work of Sigmund Freud*, Basic Books, New York. There are at least two collections of letters from Freud to read: edited by Jeffrey M. Masson (1986), *The Complete Letters to Wilhelm Fliess, 1887–1904*, Harvard University Press, Cambridge, MA; and *The Freud/Jung Letters: The Correspondence between Sigmund Freud and C. G. Jung*, Princeton University Press, Princeton, NJ, 1994.

Of Freud's works, of course you can't help but browse *The Interpretation of Dreams*, Wordsworth Editions, 1997. Among the most accessible essays are *The Psychopathology of Everyday Life*, Penguin Classics, London, 2002, the clinical case of Dora (*Case Histories I: "Dora" and "Little Hans"*, Penguin Books, London, 1990), *A General Introduction to Psychoanalysis*, CreateSpace, 2016.

To get closer to Melanie Klein we suggest: Hanna Segal (1988), *Introduction to the Work of Melanie Klein*, Karnac, London; Phyllis Grosskurth (1987), *Melanie Klein: Her World and Her Work*, Karnac, London; and finally Julia Kristeva (2004), *Melanie Klein*, Columbia University Press, New York.

Donald Winnicott's delicious (1964), *The Child, the Family, and the Outside World*, Penguin, Harmondsworth, is a must.

For Wilfred R. Bion, a brilliant but difficult author, perhaps we can start with the clinical seminars: *The Italian Seminars*, Routledge, London, 2005 and

The Tavistock Seminars, Routledge, London, 2005. We also recommend Leon Grinberg, Dario Sor, Elisabeth Tabak de Bianchedi, *Introduction to the Work of Bion*; and Joan Symington, Neville Symington (1996), *The Clinical Thinking of Wilfred Bion*, Routledge, London.

On the relationship between psychoanalysis and philosophy we suggest to scroll through the various essays in *The Italian Psychoanalytic Annual* dedicated to Maurice Merleau-Ponty (9/2015), Martin Heidegger (10/2016) and Ludwig Wittgenstein (11/2017).

Very useful dictionaries to move between terms and concepts of psycho-analysis are: Jean Laplanche, Jean-Bertrand Pontalis (1988), *The Language of Psychoanalysis*, Routledge, London; Claude Le Guen (2018), *Dictionnaire Freudien*, PUF, Paris.

Among the psychoanalytic manuals we suggest: Antonino Ferro (ed.) (2018), *Contemporary Bionian Theory and Technique in Psychoanalysis*, Routledge, London; and *Psychoanalytic Practice Today: A Post-Bionian Introduction to Psychopathology, Affect and Emotions*, Routledge, London, 2019; Anthony Elliott, Jeffrey Pragier (eds) (2016), *The Routledge Handbook of Psychoanalysis in the Social Sciences and Humanities*, Routledge, London.

For the theory of the analytical field, by Antonino Ferro:

The Bi-Personal Field: Experiences in Child Analysis. Routledge, London, 1999; *Seeds of Illness, Seeds of Recovery*. Routledge, London, 2004; *Psychoanalysis as Therapy and Storytelling* 2006; *Avoiding Emotions, Living Emotions*, Routledge, London, 2011; *Mind Works: Technique and Creativity in Psychoanalysis*, Routledge, London, 2009; *Torments of the Soul: Psychoanalytic Transformations in Dreaming and Narration*, Routledge, London, 2015; *Psychoanalysis and Dreams: Bion, the Field and the Viscera of the Mind*, 2019; *The New Analyst's Guide to the Galaxy: Questions about Contemporary Psychoanalysis*, Karnac, London, 2017; Ferro, A., and Basile, R. (eds) (2009) *The Analytic Field: A Clinical Concept*. Karnac, London.

And by Giuseppe Civitarese:

The Intimate Room: Theory and Technique of the Analytic Field, Routledge, London, 2010; *The Violence of Emotions: Bion and Post-Bionian Psychoanalysis*, Routledge, London, 2012; *The Necessary Dream: New Theories and Techniques of Interpretation in Psychoanalysis*, Routledge, London, 2014; *Losing Your Head: Abjection, Aesthetic Conflict and Psychoanalytic Criticism*, Rowman & Littlefield, Lanham, MD, 2015; *The Analytic Field and its Transformations* (with A. Ferro), Routledge, London 2015; *Truth and the Unconscious*, Routledge, London 2016; *An Apocryphal Dictionary of Psychoanalysis*, Routledge, London 2019; *Sublime Subjects: Aesthetic Experience and Intersubjectivity in Psychoanalysis*, Routledge, London 2018; (ed.) *Bion and Contemporary Psychoanalysis: Reading A Memoir of the Future*, Routledge, London 2018; (with H. Levine, eds): *The W. R. Bion Tradition: Lines of Development—Evolution of Theory and Practice over the Decades*, Karnac, London 2015; (with M. Katz and R. Cassorla (eds) (2016), *Advances in Contemporary Psychoanalytic Field Theory: Concept and Future Development (Psychoanalytic Field Theory Book series)*, Routledge, London.)

REFERENCES

Barthes R. (1977), *Fragments D'un Discours Amoureux*, Éditions du Seuil, Paris (trad. it.) *Il discorso amoroso. Seminario a l'École Pratique des Hautes Études 1974–1776, seguito da Frammenti di un discorso amoroso (inediti)*, Mimesis, Milano-Udine 2015.

Bion W.R. (1955), The development of schizophrenic thought, *Second Thoughts*, Heinemann, London, pp. 36–42.

Bion W.R. (1962), The psycho-analytic study of thinking, *International Journal of Psycho-Analysis*, 43, pp. 306–310.

Bion W.R. (1992), *Cogitations*, Karnac, London.

Bléandonu G. (1990), *Wilfred Bion: His Life and Works*, Other Press, New York, 1999.

Blum H.P. (1999), Reflections on Freud's letter from Florence, 24 September 7, 1896, *Journal of the American Psychoanalytic Association*, 47, pp. 1249–1252.

Bollas C. (1987), *The Shadow of the Object: Psychoanalysis of the Unthought Known*, Columbia University Press, New York.

Chetrit-Vatine V. (2012), *The Ethical Seduction of the Analytic Situation: The Feminine-Maternal Origins of Responsibility for the Other*, Routledge, London 2014.

Civitarese G. (2008), *The Intimate Room. Theory and Technique of the Analytic Field*, Routledge, London 2010.

Civitarese G. (2011), Caesura as Bion's discourse on method, *The Violence of Emotions: Bion and Post-Bionian Psychoanalysis*, Routledge, London 2012, pp. 8–33.

Edelman G. (1992), *Bright Air, Brilliant Fire: On the Matter of the Mind*, Basic Books, New York.

Ellenberger H.F. (1970), *The Discovery of the Unconscious: The History and Evolution of Dynamic Psychiatry*, Basic Books, New York.

Ferro A. (1992), *The Bi-Personal Field*, Routledge, London 1999.

Ferro A. (ed.) (2013), *Contemporary Bionian Theory and Technique in Psychoanalysis*, Routledge, London 2018.

Freud S. (1892–5), Studies on hysteria, *The Standard Edition, Volume 2*.

Freud S. (1895), (1895a) Project for a scientific psychology, *The Standard Edition, Volume 1*, Hogarth Press, London, pp. 295–397.

Freud S. (1909), Five lectures on psycho-analysis, *The Standard Edition, Volume 11*, Hogarth Press, London 1957, pp. 3–55.

Freud S. (1912), Recommendations to physicians practising psycho-analysis, *The Standard Edition, Volume 12 (1911–1913): The Case of Schreber, Papers on Technique and Other Works*, pp. 109–120.

Freud S. (1914a), Remembering, repeating and working-through, *The Standard Edition, Volume 12*, Hogarth Press, London 1958.

Freud S. (1914c), (1918) from the history of an infantile neurosis, *The Standard Edition, Volume 18*.

Freud S. (1920), Beyond the pleasure principle, *The Standard Edition, Volume 18*.

Freud S. (1921), Group psychology and the analysis of the ego, *The Standard Edition, Volume 18 (1920–1922): Beyond the Pleasure Principle, Group Psychology and Other Works*, pp. 65–144.

Freud S. (1929), (1930). Civilization and its discontents, *The Standard Edition, Volume 21 (1927–1931): The Future of an Illusion, Civilization and Its Discontents, and Other Works*, pp. 57–146.

Ginzburg C. (1986), *Clues, Myths, and the Historical Method*, Johns Hopkins University Press, Baltimore, 2013.

Greenson R. (1967), *The Technique and Practice of Psychoanalysis*, International Universities Press, New York.

Grotstein J. (2007), *A Beam of Intense Darkness: Wilfred Bion's Legacy to Psychoanalysis*, Karnac, London.

Haddad A., Haddad G. (1995), *Freud En Italie: Psychanalyse Du Voyage*, Albin Michel, Paris.

Jelloun T.B. (2001), *This Blinding Absence of Light*, trans. Coverdale L., Penguin Books, London 2006.

Jones E. (1953), *Sigmund Freud: Life and Work*, Hogarth Press, London.

Keats J. (1819), *Ode on a Grecian Urn*.

Kernberg O.F. (2011), Divergent contemporary trends in psychoanalytic theory, *Psychoanalytic Review Journal*, 98, pp. 633–664.

King P., Steiner R. (eds) (1991), *The Freud-Klein Controversies 1941–45*, Routledge, London and New York.

Klein M. (1927), The psychological principles of infant analysis, *International Journal of Psycho-analysis*, 8, pp. 25–37.

Klein M. (1932), *The Psychoanalysis of Children*, Hogarth Press, London.

Kojève A. (1947), *Introduction to the Reading of Hegel: Lectures on the Phenomenology of Spirit*, Cornell University Press, New York, 1980.

Kristeva J. (1983), *Tales of Love* (trans. Léon Roudiez, 1987), Columbia University Press, New York.

Kristeva J. (1985), *In the Beginning Was Love: Psychoanalysis and Faith* (trans. Arthur Goldhammer, 1988), Columbia University Press, New York.

Kristeva J. (2003), *Melanie Klein*, Columbia University Press, New York 2004.

Kuhn T.S. (1962), *The Structure of Scientific Revolutions*, The University of Chicago Press, Chicago.

Lacan J. (1947), La psychiatrie anglaise et la guerre, *L'Évolution Psychiatrique*, iii, pp. 293–312.

Lai G. (1985), *La Conversazione felice*, Il Saggiatore, Milano.

Laplanche J., Pontalis J. B. (1967), *The Language of Psycho-Analysis*, W. W. Norton & Company, New York, 1974.

Le Guen C. (2008), *Dictionnaire Freudien*, Presses Universitaires de France, Paris.

Levine S.Z. (2008), *Lacan Reframed*, Tauris, London.

Milner M. (1950), *On Not Being Able to Paint*, Heinemann, London.

Nancy J.L. (1996), *Être Singulier Pluriel*, Éditions Galilée, Paris.

Ogden, T.H. (1991). Some Theoretical Comments on Personal Isolation. *Psychonal. Dial.*, 1(3), pp. 377–390.

Ogden T.H. (1994), *Subjects of Analysis*, Karnac, London.

Ogden, T.H. (2007), Reading Harold Searles. *International Journal of Psycho-Analysis.*, 88(2), pp. 353–369.

Ogden T.H. (2008), *Rediscovering Psychoanalysis: Thinking and Feeling, Learning and Forgetting*, Routledge, New York.

Ricoeur P. (1965), *Freud and Philosophy: An Essay on Interpretation*, trans. Denis Savage. Yale University Press, New Haven 1970 (1965).

Salomonsson B. (2014), *Psychoanalytic Therapy with Infants and Their Parents: Practice, Theory, and Results*, Routledge, New York.

Searles H. (1965), *Collected Papers on Schizophrenia and Related Subjects*, International Universities Press, New York.

Steiner J. (2016), Illusion, disillusion, and irony in psychoanalysis, *The Psychoanalytic Quarterly*, pp. 427–447.

Tarizzo D. (2009), *Introduzione a Lacan*, Roma-Bari, Laterza.

Trotter W. (2009), *Instincts of the Herd in Peace and War* (1916), Cornell University Library, Ithaca, NY.

Vygotskij L., Lurija A. (1984), *Orudie i znak v razvitii rebënka Sobranieso.inenij*, vol. vi, Pedagogika, Moskwa (trans. Italian *Strumento e segno nello sviluppo del bambino*, Laterza, Roma-Bari 1997).

Weiss E. (1931), *Elementi di psicoanalisi*, Hoepli, Milano.

Westen D. (1999), The scientific status of unconscious processes, *Journal of the American Psychoanalytic Association*, 47, pp. 1061–1106.

Winnicott D.W. (1949), Hate in countertransference, *International Journal of Psychoanalysis*, 30: 69–74.

Winnicott D.W. (1958), *Through Paediatrics to Psycho-Analysis*, Tavistock, London.

Winnicott D.W. (1964), *The Child, the Family, and the outside World*, Penguin, Harmondsworth.

Winnicott D.W. (1965), *The Maturational Process and the Facilitating Environment: Studies in the Theory of Emotional Development*, Hogarth, London.

Winnicott D.W. (1971), *Playing and Reality*, Tavistock, London.

Winnicott, D.W. (1975). *Through Paediatrics to Psycho-Analysis*, pp. 1–325. London, The Hogarth Press and the Institute of Psycho-Anlysis.

Winnicott D.W. (1989), *Psycho-analytic Explorations*, Karnac, London.

INDEX

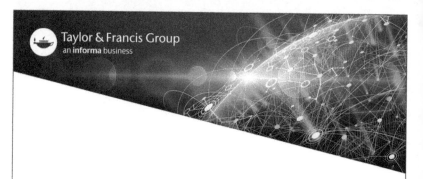